Advanced Praise

This wonderful book from the pen of Donna Mathiowetz is an essential read for every person who dares to love. It will first inspire you to believe grief is survivable, as it tells a family's story of tragic loss. Their loss, well grieved, opens and deepens their lives rather than bringing destruction or closing them to loving yet again. From their own amazing journey, great wisdom is gleaned and gently imparted that will equip the reader to appropriately support others as they traverse grief's path while imparting the wisdom and skills we will inevitably need in walking those paths ourselves. We all need these skills!
—Pastor Jim Anderson, The Harbor Church

Donna's story is one of perseverance, growth and grace. In this book, she shares her family's story, allowing the memory of her loved ones to live on, but also to help ease the heartache of others. Though many events in her life are chronicled in this book, her legacy will not be one of sadness, but one of hope and healing. Her story, along with the lessons she has learned, provide hope, resources and sense of community for those who have experienced loss.

—**Melissa Stevens Freiermuth**

What Have You Done Since I Left?

Live fully in
Mark's place

Donna

Isaiah 41:10

What Have You Done Since I Left?

Donna Mathiowetz

Minneapolis, Minnesota

First edition
Published 2020
Printed in the United States of America
ISBN: 978-1-952976-01-8
Library of Congress Control Number: 2020911613

Cover Design & Interior Book Design: Ann Aubitz
Jackie Deems, © 1989 – used with permission

For more information contact:

Kirk House Publishers
1250 E 115th Street
Burnsville, MN 55337
612-781-2815

Dedication

I dedicate this book to my three grandchildren,
Emma, Ean and Ellie.
I hope you will share this with your children someday.
I also want to dedicate it to my children, Jill and Brandon,
Timm and Oleg.
All of you gave me a reason to write this book.

Acknowledgements

Thank you to my husband Dick, who faithfully encouraged me to complete this even when I wasn't sure I would. I'm grateful to Connie Anderson whose editing helped to make it all flow. Thank you Ann Aubitz for your patience and guidance throughout the project. Gloria VanDemmeltraadt and Melissa Freiermuth, thank you for your proofreading expertise. I certainly appreciate those of you who have your own stories, entrusted them to me and then allowed me to share them.

Table of Contents

PART I..11

  1. Our Many "Leaps of Faith"............................13

  2. The Day Everything Changed........................21

  3. Dick's Long Trip Home 27

  4. The Power of Prayer 31

  5. Forgiveness...A Simple Word with Such Impact
    33

  6. Bitter or Better...37

  7. The "Something Good" 41

  8. The Things We Hold Onto............................47

  9. We Know That in All Things... 51

Part II..57

  10. Oleg's Brief but Impactful Life 59

  11. The United Nation Comes to Hastings 73

  12. Brandon's Extended Hospital Stay 81

Part III 89

  13. The Empty Nest 91

  14. Bittersweet Memories 97

Part IV 105

    15. Come Alongside 107

    16. Meaning...Purpose...Hope............................131

Part V 135

    17. The Resiliency Factor 137

    18. Not Normal...But Better 145

Final Thoughts.. 149

Recommendations 151

About the Author 151

PART I

Timm's Story

Chapter 1

Our Many "Leaps of Faith"

This was us in 1972

Have you ever looked back at where you've been to appreciate how far you've come? My husband, Dick, and I were two of six adults and about sixty youth packed into a yellow school bus heading to ski at Bridger Bowl in Bozeman, Montana. We were praying for a safe and fun weekend. Little did we know how much our lives would be impacted a week later.

While on this long, long bus ride, my mind had time to wander, and I thought about the giant leap of faith that Dick and I had made in November 1972, getting married when I was only seventeen—and pregnant. In two-and-a-half years, we had two children, Jill and Timm. Dick traveled five days a week, and we were far from our family or hometown. This forced us to rely on each other and grow as a couple.

Leaping ahead with faith that I could accomplish more than many people thought, I completed my required classes to earn my high school diploma. I finished my junior year before Jill was born in May and completed my senior year via a correspondence course. My hard work and determination gave me the opportunity to walk across the stage with my classmates and receive my diploma, while hearing Jill's little voice in the audience enthusiastically calling out, "Mommy, Mommy!"

I didn't know it at the time, but it was a major step that would give me the courage and confidence to face and conquer other challenging times ahead. More often than not, the times we look back on as difficult become the times that have prepared us for our futures. In our "want-everything-now" instant world, it would do us good sometimes to understand that there will be seasons that require more from us.

These times call for more time,
more patience, and more willingness
to trust that there is one greater than
ourselves who is preparing us
for what lies ahead.

With more time for daydreaming between conversations on the bus, I found myself thinking about my Grandpa Ernie. At any age, thinking back to a time you realized you had lost something or someone important to you can be healthy. It may have been something of value like a special gift you received or maybe it was the death of a beloved person. Your loss may have been from a long time ago, or maybe just last week. Reflecting on challenging times in our lives can help to reassure us that we can survive those yet to come.

My first significant loss occurred in 1976 when my Grandpa Ernie died. He had endured several strokes while only in his sixties. Finally, a major stroke put him in a nursing home where he stayed for eleven long years, unable to speak or walk and barely feed himself. So, when he died, I had mixed emotions. Part of me was sad because Grandpa Ernie and I had a sweet relationship. But a bigger part of my heart felt relief for him. Grandpa Ernie wasn't suffering anymore. He had been freed.

❖

Feelings of relief are not uncommon.
This topic often comes up in the
grief support group that Dick and I lead,
probably because it's a safe place to share
something that could be misunderstood
out in the world.

Many who have been caregivers for their terminally ill friend or family member have experienced this. It seems that a burden is lifted when they realize they are not alone in being relieved that this person is no longer suffering. But there can also be a loss of purpose. After the death, what they needed to get up for each day is no longer there. It's a sudden change that requires the caregiver to find new purpose while they grieve their loss.

Losing loved ones is always difficult. My husband's and my own families have had their share. We have endured the pain of losing two young nephews. Christopher was twenty-one when he died by suicide, and Danny age thirty-one, due to a blood disease complicated by alcohol abuse. Watching their parents navigate the rocky terrain of unspeakable loss was heart-wrenching. Even though I was years ahead of them, there was little I could do to ease their pain.

Chris   Danny

❖

Grief will occur whenever we lose
something or someone of great value to us.
The duration and intensity will
differ depending on the depth of the
relationship and nature of the loss.

A Little Trip Down Memory Lane:
February 1992

Every other year a few of the area churches would organize this youth ski trip to Bridger Bowl. Dick and I stepped up to be part of the leadership team. Timm and a couple friends decided to join us. Nothing says bonding quite like a road trip on a crowded bus. We had two full days of amazing spring skiing that February of 1992, including the Leap Year's extra day. Those two days gave Dick and me the opportunity to spend time with sixteen-year-old Timm. The three of us would hop on a chairlift to begin the twenty-minute trip up that beautiful mountain in Bozeman Montana.

During those times we talked about how things were going. Timm had come through some tumultuous teen years and was looking forward to brighter days. He was smart and athletic with a winsome personality. Timm was popular and handsome...and he knew it. He also tended to live life on the edge and wasn't afraid to take a few risks from time to time. Some of the trips up the ski lift were just spent in awe of the grandeur around us. When we reached the top, Timm would often ski down with his friends while Mom and Dad preferred something less threatening than a Black Diamond hill. I recall one descent when he chose to stay with us. Timm and I had gone down to a certain point and turned to see where Dick was. What we saw was him, bombing the hill, obviously much faster than his experience would allow. We knew this may not end well.

In an instant, Dick came near us, and then in an effort to slow down, he headed for the chest-high powder (and a few trees) at the edge of the groomed trail. He went in far enough so that Timm and I couldn't even see him. Worried, we looked at each other. Then Timm, with trepidation hollered "Dad, are you okay?" Thankfully, without much delay, Dick responded, in a disgusted tone, "Yes, I'll meet you at the bottom!"

The weather allowed us to sit at the picnic tables outside the chalet. It took what seemed like a long time before Dick appeared to join us for lunch. Timm was still laughing at what he had seen. It was even funnier when Dick explained that his plan up on the slope was to get to where Timm and I were waiting, and do a quick stop as he turned in order to spray us with snow. Instead he spent about twenty minutes working to escape the soft powder that had enveloped him.

We had appropriately chosen "Leap of Faith" as the theme for our trip. Each evening, we would go into our small groups to discuss whatever topic was presented by our Youth Pastor, Gordon. Being in those surroundings, and away from the obligations of everyday life, put all of us into a different state of mind. Timm was in awe of how Gordon could break down God's word and promises into language he could understand and accept. Betty, who facilitated the small group Timm was in, remembers that he seemed relaxed and accepting of what all this "faith" stuff meant for him. He asked questions and received answers *that assured him that he was loved and forgiven by God just as he was.*

Little did we know how vital all that "faith" stuff
would be to him and us in the days ahead.

Timm and Paul at Bridger Bowl

Chapter 2
The Day Everything Changed

My favorite picture of Timm

March 6, 1992

We had just returned from Montana five days earlier. Spring was still a few weeks away in Minnesota, where my family lived. My sister and her husband had planned a ski weekend in Tahoe, and I would be taking care of Dillon and Derek, ages two and eight, while they were away. Earlier in the week, Dick had gone to our hometown, 110 miles away, where he would stay at my parents' house while he and my dad overhauled his work van. Our daughter Jill had moved to her first apartment in Hastings, Minnesota. She would watch the boys until I picked them up after work that Friday afternoon.

When I returned home with the little guys in tow, it was evident that Timm and a few friends had been there after school. Some dishes in the sink indicated they had enjoyed an after-school snack. We had a spiral-bound notebook on the kitchen island that we used to let each other know our plans. His note said he was planning to go to a movie with friends but would check in with me later. I made dinner for the little boys and we made plans for a fun outing the next day. Timm called around eight o'clock. He asked if he could spend the night at one of his friend's homes and plan to be home by ten in the morning to join the boys and me for some fun. I asked about curfew time and said I would check with the other mom, and he should call to confirm the plan with me.

Instead, the next two calls I answered were from a couple of girls asking if I had heard from Timm. I told them I had talked to him, and that he was going to a movie. When the phone rang the third time, I heard a lot of loud voices and some crying in the background. The caller was very distressed as she told me she heard that Timm had been shot—and then she hung up.

My immediate defense was to go into denial. Surely, that was some crazy rumor being shared among a group of teenagers with no real way of knowing what had really happened. I didn't know what to do. After a few minutes, I decided to call our local hospital to inquire whether anyone had been brought in recently. At that time, Hastings' population was only 10,000, so my question was relevant. The ER nurse's answer created a chill that went up my spine as he replied, "We had only one come in—and that was a DOA." I knew that meant Dead on Arrival.

What am I supposed to do now? Who do I call? That certainly wasn't Timm! I felt my heart beginning to race as I picked up the phone to call the sheriff's department. I knew Timm was five miles outside of town, so if something had happened, they would know. I explained why I was calling, relaying the very little that I knew at that moment. There was a pause at the other end of the line, and then I was told they would need to put me on hold. After what seemed like an eternity, the deputy returned and said someone would get back to me after they looked into it. *Into what*, I wondered.

My nephews were fast asleep in the next room so I couldn't follow my strong desire to get in the car and drive out to where I thought Timm might be. I believe that was God's way of protecting me from what I would have found. Soon, several teens were at my door, and more were close behind them. They were crying...some were wailing, certain that the news they had heard was true. Not only had Timm been shot, *but he was dead*!

I continued to refuse to believe it. I had no confirmation from the authorities. With some of Jill and Timm's friends now there to stay with the boys, I was going to go to where I could find out for myself. Just as I was heading out the door, I was met by a sheriff's deputy and a woman standing on the steps, who was introduced as the Dakota County Coroner. That still plays out in my mind like a scene from a movie.

My head knew what that meant, but my heart refused to allow it to be true. They came into the kitchen. The coroner looked at the pictures displayed on the refrigerator next to her. She said, "Yes, that's him. Then she turned to me and said, "And he still looks like that." I crumbled to the floor with feelings I had never experienced before or since. We sat at the kitchen table as she explained to me as much as she could. Our sixteen-year-old son, Timm had been shot and killed by an acquaintance at a party, the result of a shot to his left temple, at close range. The combination of beer, poor judgment, and very careless handling of a .44 caliber magnum handgun changed our lives forever.

The minutes and hours that followed are still etched in my mind decades later. At times it seems like yesterday, although it feels like forever since I've felt a hug from Timm's strong arms. I really don't remember what else the coroner said as I sat there in total shock and disbelief. I do recall saying to her, "You have a terrible job!"

Chapter 3

Dick's Long Trip Home

I never did know who made the call to my parents' house that night. Dick had already been sleeping for an hour when he was awoken by my mom and dad standing over him. They told him he needed to get up and go home. Timm had been shot and killed. He, of course, remembers the details of that night like it was yesterday. Mom and Dad went back upstairs as he jumped out of bed. He took the time to fold up the hide-a-bed and blankets and then went upstairs. He told my dad he'd need to borrow his car as his van was still in the shop across the street. Another plan was already in progress.

The entire third of the state was blanketed in an extremely heavy fog which sometimes occurs in the very early spring. I was adamant that Dick shouldn't drive home alone, even if it hadn't been foggy. Arrangements were made quickly for Dick to be brought home by way of being transported from one county line to the next by the various sheriff's deputies along the 110-mile trip back to Hastings. A deputy was already waiting in the driveway to begin what would turn out to be a much longer drive than ever before. We had made that trip dozens of times, taking us about two hours and fifteen minutes. That night it would take Dick four-and-a-half hours.

There was no conversation as he sat in the caged backseat of those sheriff cars because the drivers were all white-knuckling it to reach their next rendezvous point. The visibility was down to just inches at times. Dick sat there with only his own thoughts racing through his mind. All he knew was that Timm had been shot and killed. He wrestled with God in that back seat. He was telling Him, "I cannot do this!" "How am I supposed to handle this?" "If I do this my way, it's not going to be good for anyone!" After a while, he sensed God's answer in his spirit.

What he heard Him say was,
"Hand over the destructive anger.
Give it to me to bear for you."

So finally, at 4:20 a.m., the long, agonizing trip came to an end as the car pulled into the driveway of our home. Someone told me he was home and Jill and I went to greet him. He looked as if he'd seen a ghost, and I'm certain we looked the same. We held each other while all those around us cried with us. Soon, all the people who had gathered to support us and each other began to leave. Jill wanted to go to her apartment for a while to rest as best she could, leaving Dick and me to begin to grapple with what had just transpired in the last five horrendous hours of our lives.

Chapter 4

The Power of Prayer

Timm's life had ended just eight hours before. As the sun was about to rise on that Saturday morning, we sat together in the living room. We were prompted to hold hands and pray this prayer. It was short and simple.

"Dear Lord, please take the destructive anger from us. Amen"
What we came to realize as the weeks, months and years
unfolded in front of us is that He did just that.

What I always want people to understand as I share this crucial part of our story is that it is about *destructive anger*. Anger itself is a God-given emotion. Even Jesus became angry. Oftentimes anger can be the catalyst needed to affect change when channeled constructively. The anger I speak of is the kind of anger that only causes more destruction and pain to the bearer as well as to those around him or her. Even in our numbness, in our spirit we knew we wanted to do whatever we could to make sure we didn't lose more than we already had.

At risk were several things, one of them being our marriage. Within the first few weeks of our loss, one of our pastors shared the higher-than-average rate of divorce among couples after the death of a child. We also had to do all we could to be there for our daughter, and to model what healthy grieving looks like as best we could. Many other kids and teens needed us as well.

We discovered that one of the most important things we learned to do was to let each other grieve as we needed, no matter how painful it may be to watch.

I couldn't fix it for Dick. He couldn't make it better for me—so we mutually respected each other's space and time needed to actively grieve. There were many times when Dick would come home at the end of the day to hear me downstairs in Timm's room crying until I couldn't cry any more. He didn't try to tell me to stop or attempt to divert my attention to something else. He just let me grieve. I needed to do the same for him many times as well. Since then, we continue to be understanding and supportive of each other when we say we're "having a Timmy time."

I can do all things through Him who gives me strength.
Philippians 4:13

Chapter 5

Forgiveness...A Simple Word with Such Impact

Summer 1992

As the months went by, I had moments when I sensed being held in Jesus' arms. I understood He didn't choose for this to happen, but I also recognized that He didn't stop it. Why...why? I spent some time, as most people who suffer a tragic loss do, asking this question. It didn't take long to realize *that there was no one who could answer it to my satisfaction.*

Over time, God guided me to replace the "why?" with "what now?" I had grasped onto and believed what Romans 8:28 tells us. "We know that in all things God works for the good of those who love Him, who have been called according to His purpose."

God's purpose for my life began with baby steps as I was able.

❖

The journey of grief is a marathon, not a sprint.

As I educated myself about this uninvited visitor in our lives, I learned of the importance of taking care of myself emotionally, mentally, spiritually, and physically. I had enjoyed taking long walks before Timm's death and resumed it soon afterward, realizing that it was a good way for me to clear my head and relieve some of the stress I was experiencing. I often prayed as I walked and tried to listen for something from God. He caused me to begin to think more about the young man who shot Timm, as well as considering what his family might be experiencing. Then a few steps at a time God led me down a path called "forgiveness."

After a few months, my husband and I had been given the courage and strength to forgive. It was most certainly not in our own power, but with the help of God.

The forgiveness came in three areas:

First, we chose to forgive ourselves for anything we didn't do right as parents. It seems that whenever our children stray off the path that we have paved it is natural to question yourself. *What did we miss...what didn't we say or do?*

Secondly, we forgave Timm for the lack of judgment he demonstrated that night. It wasn't the first bad decision he had made, but it would become his last.

Then, finally we chose to forgive the nineteen-year-old man who shot him. Forgive us our trespasses as we forgive those who trespass against us.

I wrote the young man a letter while he was imprisoned for his crime to express our forgiveness. We didn't condone his actions, but we forgave him as God has numerous times forgiven us. Choosing to forgive enabled us to continue on our grief journey without the heavy burden of unforgiveness.

Because we chose to forgive, we have been more able to use this life experience to be there for others as they face similar challenges.

Grief...Forgiveness...Healing—it takes time.

Chapter 6

Bitter or Better

It seems that with every tragic twist and turn in life, we all are given the choice to concentrate *only on what we've lost* or to eventually, in time, choose to receive that which will add richness and joy back into our lives. Will we choose to be bitter or become better?

I clearly remember the day when I made a choice. It was a choice that I believe with all my heart was one that changed the trajectory of my life as well as that of many others. As I was coming home from running errands, I came to a stop sign, a place I had been a hundred times before. I had a choice to go right or left; I thought of it as a fork in the road. With no cars behind me, I was able to sit there for a bit and contemplate this visual that God had given me. It represented a choice I needed to make in my own life.

If going left would lead me to a "Bitter Life" and going right would be the "Better Life," which would I choose?

Similar to the decision I had made to forgive, the choice I made to choose "Better" over "Bitter" resulted in a life that testifies to the power of both. Just as forgiveness didn't make my grief disappear, neither did choosing to live a Better Life. It simply allowed the heavy burden of the life—halting kind of grief—to be lifted from my back.

If you know someone who carries the load of unforgiveness or bitterness in their lives, it is ultimately a choice they have made. The good news is it's never too late to make the decision to change that. Is it easy? No. Will they need some help? Quite possibly.

❖

Anyone can get stuck in the place of continuing to focus only on what we have lost.

I was stuck there for a while.
Yes...

- We lost our son, brother, brother-in-law, and an uncle.
- We lost our future daughter and sister-in-law.
- We lost our future grandchildren, cousins, nieces, and nephews.
- We would not have Timm there to help us as we age.

But at the same time, and in the months and years that followed, we chose to receive:
- Love and support from our family and friends
- Empathy and understanding
- The ability to forgive
- An abundant life
- The desire to let God make good come from something tragic and painful
- Compassion for others who are new to this thing called grief

There is no doubt that loss and grief changes each of us in some way. Traumatic loss, even more so. I also know that these changes don't have to be a negative. I see more compassion and understanding in us. We tend to not get all caught up in the minutia of life. Those are all good changes that often can guide us to a place where we can and want to help someone else whose grief journey has just begun.

Those whose lives are altered in such a major way often move forward to become people who, because of what they have lost, can love in a new way.

Chapter 7

The "Something Good"

About five years after Timm's death, a few people came together to start a grief support group in our hometown of Hastings, Minnesota. Dick and I knew that we could help and were eager to see this much-needed resource become available in our little town. It featured a speaker each week who presented a thirty-minute educational piece on some aspect of grief. The speakers ranged from those who would share their own journey to pastors who would help us to understand how faith and grief can coexist. Others helped us to understand how grief affects our bodies and minds. That was followed by an hour of small group discussion time, guided by a more seasoned member of the group. For so many, this became a lifeline. It was the one place they could come and be real and have no one judge them.

He comes alongside us when we go through hard times, and before
you know it, He brings us alongside someone else who is going
through hard times so we can be there for that
person just as God was there for us.
2 Corinthians 1:4

I continued to speak for that group for the next twenty years, and Dick I were small group guides as well. As we observed so many begin to heal and learning to adjust to their "new normal", I know it was another part of our own healing as well.

❖

So take a new grip with your tired hands and stand
firm on your shaky legs.
Mark out a straight path for your feet.
Then those who follow you, though they are weak and lame, will
not stumble and fall but will become strong.
Hebrews 12: 12-13

A few years ago, Marty and Lila, the two faithful women who had done most of the heavy lifting for the group were both retiring. When it looked like the group could possibly end, Dick and I decided to take it on. We believed it was too vital a resource to let go. We simplified it a bit, meeting twice a month and using some videos for the education as well as a few speakers and myself. We usually have about fifteen to twenty people for each gathering, most of them women and a few brave men who have lost their spouses.

Our conversations are varied as we try to go with the flow of what the particular needs are at each meeting. A common topic is discussing what the loved ones we've lost would want for our lives after they're gone. It was during one of those times that Dick found himself removed from the actual discussion, and saw this little scenario being played out in his mind. He saw himself entering Heaven and being greeted by Timm. There was as exuberant reunion and then they sat down at a table, across from each other. Timm reached for his dad's hands and with wide eyes and great anticipation he said, "Dad, tell me everything you've done since I left!"

I often close my presentations with this story and ask the other participants to contemplate how they would want to answer that question, if asked, when they reunite with their loved one.

Given all the experience I had gleaned from walking alongside so many others in grief, I knew it was time to take the next step. This book you are holding in your hand is one of those steps. So often when I have shared even part of our life story with others, I hear, "You need to write a book." My response has been, "Yes, I know, I'm working on it." A big part of my desire to write this book was to make sure that our story, in my own words, would be there long after we're gone. It is our legacy for our grandchildren and others as well.

This is the story of our Christian faith, and the power of prayer, and forgiveness.

I had partial chapters written in my mind, but only a few were on paper. I also knew I wanted to do more speaking, but not only in grief support groups. In April 2017 as I was doing my morning devotions and praying for the Lord's direction for what I should be doing, His still small voice spoke to me once again. He said, "If not now, when?" At sixty-three, I felt a sense of urgency to get serious about whatever God's plan was. I knew that if it was His will, the right doors would open. People entered my life who had the knowledge and tools that I didn't. I quickly wrote a guided journal titled, *A Journal for Your Journey* and created a deck of *Journey Cards*. Some of the speaking engagements have come from unexpected sources. Life Source, the organ procurement organization in Minneapolis, hired me to be their keynote speaker for their annual Donor Family Gathering. I have shared our story with Senior Living Communities, realtors, women's business groups, church groups, services of remembrance, and of course grief support groups. How can I add value to the lives of a group of realtors or businesswomen?

What I know is that everyone who
loses something or someone of
great value will experience grief
and loss at some point in their lives.

The depth and breadth of the losses vary. Often a less traumatic loss will cause a larger loss from the past, never dealt with, to surface. Some of the feelings can be the same.

When speaking to a business group, I share some of what I've learned on my journey, but there's more. Our culture has so much to understand and apply when it comes to supporting someone else in grief. I pose this question to many of the groups. "Would you like to be more comfortable at knowing what to say or do...and what *not* to say or do?" The responses have always been ones of gratitude for what I was able to share with them. I know most people want to help, but often just don't know how.

Knowing how underserved the parents who have lost a child are, I created a five-week series called "Gone Too Soon." It is specifically for parents and grandparents who have lost a child. We meet each week. I share a thirty to forty minute education piece and then we break into small groups for discussion time with guides who have also lost a child. Dick leads the men's group and we have three to four females for the women, in groups of six to eight members. So far, we have conducted these in different cities with good results. There were twenty-five participants at one and forty at another, and thankfully the majority came as couples.

I find that grieving parents are so hungry for a place where everyone understands each other.

Recently, we expanded our outreach to our grieving community by providing a twice a month, separate ninety-minute meeting just for grieving parents. Many lives have been touched through this ministry.

In most cases parents who lose a child,
find that a general grief group
isn't the right setting to address their unique needs.

The specific challenges of the death of a child are so different from the loss of a spouse, parent or sibling. Anything regarding the different stages of grief simply don't apply. It has been said that when we lose a spouse, we lose the past, when we lose a child, we have lost the future.

Chapter 8

The Things We Hold Onto

Much of my work in this arena of loss and grief is to help normalize the process. Within the safety of support groups, questions can be asked and conversations had that wouldn't be possible with those who just don't understand. I try to be transparent and share what I know from my own journey. The things that become treasures to us after a loved one dies is a topic that seems to bring an assurance of normalcy to most everyone. Most often, it's not even a special piece of jewelry or Grandma's favorite vase. This may be especially true when a child dies. Sometimes the items left behind can bring a smile and give us an opportunity to share a story, but others only bring more pain.

Along with the many sympathy cards that were stacked on the kitchen island during those first weeks, there was something else that rendered me frozen. It was the ten death certificates that our funeral director had brought to us. They laid there for a couple of weeks. The disbelief of this reality was stifling and I needed time to accept it. In the section that contains the multiple choices for cause of death, the box next to the word *homicide* was checked. Finally, I placed them in a file right behind Timm's birth certificate with the impression of his tiny feet.

What they leave behind by way of material things may be few.

That was true for us. But here are some things we still have, decades later:

- The empty mouthwash bottle. It's still in the bottom drawer of the dresser. Timm took the last swig of it before he left for school that day.
- The now-empty Drakkar cologne bottle. It sits on top of my dresser, and every now and then I remove the cover to see if it still smells like Timm. That fragrance was ever so popular with all his buddies. If we had a few of them in our car together, it may even have required rolling down a window. We used to accuse them of showering with it.
- Finally, the chocolate syrup bottle in the refrigerator. You know the kind with the pull-up top? Timm would use his teeth to open it, even though I would often remind him that doing it was bad for his teeth. He continued to do it many times, so much that he left his tooth marks on it. So, it's still here in our

refrigerator. As needed, I will buy a fresh can of syrup, clean out the thirty-year-old bottle and refill it. The label is crinkled but my son's tooth marks are still there.

Of course, we also fondly recall our favorite memories. One of mine is when Timm was about six or seven years old. It was way too early one Christmas morning. Our bedroom was upstairs, Jill and Timm were in the lower level. I woke to a humming noise that I hadn't heard before. I woke Dick and we got up and followed the noise down the stairs.

As we peeked around the corner, we saw two small beams of light circling the family room. Timm just couldn't wait and had opened one of his gifts from under the tree. It was a remote-controlled semi-truck, headlights and all. Needless to say, Christmas morning came extra early that year.

Chapter 9

We Know That in All Things...

In my mind and heart, the blur of the next days and weeks that followed Timm's death seemed similar to the dense fog that blanketed the roads the night Dick came home. Whatever had been a normal day before was no longer attainable. One of the new normals was many of Timm's friends showing up every day after school. *We needed them and they needed us as well.* Paul, one of Timm's friends had an uncle who owned our local Dairy Queen. Shortly after Timm's death, he graciously delivered a huge box of treats that we placed in our chest freezer downstairs. As the kids came in after school, they would dash down to pick out their frozen favorite and then come back upstairs to join us at the dining room table. There we would talk and shed some tears as we opened that day's pile of sympathy cards which had been delivered. Cards, letters, and gifts of money came from many we knew, as well as from perfect strangers who had heard our story. Many had experienced losing their own child.

I remember a card that contained a $500 money order. With it was a note explaining this was money the anonymous giver hadn't expected to receive, and they felt they were to pass it on to us. The extreme generosity of family, friends, and complete strangers kept us financially afloat for several months until Dick was able to return to work. We didn't have life insurance for Timm, so the financial help we received was needed and appreciated.

FYI: Insure your children's lives.
It's affordable and can be transferred to them as adults.

As we sat around the table, often one of the kids would quietly get up and go downstairs, but not to get more ice cream. They would go to Timm's bedroom which was still like he had left it that final Friday morning. They would look through year books, check out the hockey trophies on the shelf and often just lay across his bed to cry some healing tears. Sometimes they went in pairs or alone. After a while, they would rejoin the group; no explanations needed. A few hours would pass and they would leave, but not before a tight hug and "See you tomorrow." This went on for several weeks. Then, as it needed to be, the kids regained some new normalcy in their lives.

The high school prom was just a couple months later. It was the first of what seemed like unending events that pierced my heart over and over. This would have been Timm's first prom. I visualized how handsome he would have been. Instead I saw pictures of his friends attending their prom without him. As I looked into their faces, I could see behind the required smiles the deep pain they were enduring as they grappled with what had happened.

To this day, there is a special bond between us and them. On the occasions we see them around town, there is always a warm embrace and a special look that says they have not forgotten. A small group of them continue to gather every year on the anniversary of Timm's death, and some on his birthday as well. They spend some time at the cemetery and recently invited us to join them for dinner. It was a sweet night with some laughter and a few tears as well. The bittersweet events in their lives have been many. Their graduations, weddings, and the birth of their babies and even grandbabies always trigger the thought, *I wonder what Timm's life would look like today if he were still here.*

The outpouring of love and support from so many has been and continues to be was amazing. A couple months after Timm died, a group of our daughter's friends took it upon themselves to plan a fundraiser benefit so we could put a headstones on our three graves. Our community stepped up in a big way, with silent auction items, food and music.

Some other things also stand out vividly in my memories of those early days and weeks. I remember feeling "robotic" in the first hours and days that followed. Timm had died on a Friday night. I was in my pajamas, ready to go to bed when those phone calls started coming. When the first few girls arrived at our home, I changed my clothes and my plan was to leave those girls there with my two sleeping nephews. That plan was interrupted when the sheriff and coroner arrived at the door. I know that was God's way of protecting me from seeing Timm as he lay on that cold concrete floor. Two days later I was still wearing the same sweatpants and shirt I had pulled on that night.

Someone had helped schedule the time for us to go to the funeral home to make arrangements as well as going to the cemetery to pick out a plot. One of our friends looked at me and said, "Donna, you probably should go take a shower." I complied and went downstairs to the bathroom that Timm had used just two days earlier. There was his shampoo and soap. On the vanity were his toothbrush and the empty mouthwash bottle. My numbness allowed me to observe all that, but somehow keep moving. When I came out of the bathroom, one of my friends was sitting outside the door. I wondered, *why is she sitting there?* I realized later it was because she cared and wanted to be close by should I need any help completing some-thing as simple as taking a shower. I remember people telling me that I needed to eat, but it was so difficult to swallow. It was as if my throat was lined with cotton balls.

Another couple drove us to the funeral home and then on to the cemetery. Again, in our robotic state of mind, we planned the visitation and funeral service. We walked into the room which housed all the caskets and chose the black and silver one to honor Timm's love of the LA Kings hockey team. From there we went to select the place where he would be buried. We chose a triple plot, not something most people would consider at our age.

Someone once said that intense grief
is like walking around without any skin.

There are days when it really does feel that raw. For the first few weeks I felt more protected when I was tucked away at home. I became a sponge to reading books about grief. I felt as if I had been dropped in a strange place where I didn't speak the language or have any understanding of the culture. I needed to educate myself. I wanted to understand, especially from a Christian viewpoint, how I was to navigate this rocky terrain. Some days, in between crying and then needing a nap, I would get a sliver of clarity as I did the hard work of grieving. During one of those times, I sensed the still small voice of God in my spirit. He said, "Donna, together you and I will make good come from all of this pain." I certainly didn't know when or how that might happen, but I did trust Him to do what He had promised.

Part II
Living Fully in Their Place

The greatest gift we can give to those who left us is to live fully in their place.– Unknown

Chapter 10

Oleg's Brief but Impactful Life

Oleg

18 Months After Timm's Death

❝Not at all what we have in mind" was my thought as I hung up the phone. My friend Lise had received a call from her social worker and she thought of us. In the eighteen months following Timm's death, we had been become licensed for foster care and had also completed a home study for adoption. Lise explained that a teenage boy had come from a Ukrainian orphanage to be treated for his cancer in nearby St Paul. They needed him placed in a home very soon, as the couple he was with was scheduled to leave on a mission trip shortly. The word had gone out to all the county agencies as well as the local Ukrainian communities in the Minneapolis/St Paul area.

A fifteen-year-old boy with cancer, from a foreign country and speaks no English? That was about as far from what we had envisioned as possible. Our plan *was a healthy baby.*

The slip of paper with a name and phone number for me to call if I wanted to know more was tucked away in the corner of my desk that afternoon. I told Dick about it when he came home that night. His reaction was similar to mine and we put it to rest, or so I thought.

God knew better. About a week later, I was clearing my desk of some clutter and I picked up that slip of paper. As I was about to throw it away, a nearly audible voice said very clearly, "Call the number." My prompt reply was, "Certainly by now, they have found a place for this boy!" Again, I heard, "Call the number." So, reluctantly I dialed the number while at the same time hoping I'd get an answering machine. My plan was to leave a brief message, assuming it would be the end of this. So far, so good. I left a message and at the same time tossed the slip of paper into the wastebasket thinking, "Okay Lord, I did as you asked."

Much to my surprise, my phone rang the next morning. The caller, with great emotion in her voice told me that, despite all the attempts to find a family for this boy, we were the first to even respond in any way. Jennifer asked if we would like to meet him. What could I say? I would need to talk to Dick of course, and then I'd let her know. What could we say? So, a few days later, Oleg came for a visit. With him were the couple he had been staying with and Oksana, a lovely Ukrainian woman who would serve as his translator. By this time, Oleg had experienced his first round of chemo and wasn't feeling well at all. He still knew the gravity of his situation in needing to find a home so he could remain in the U.S. and continue his treatments. He was trying so hard to be cordial and speak to us with Oksana's help. But what he really wanted to do was lay on the couch and close his eyes. We could see the helplessness in his face.

After they left Dick and I looked at each other, a bit bewildered by what we had just experienced. We began discussing the pros and cons. Yes, we were in the throes of grief. Yes, Oleg could die too. How will we communicate with him? Somehow, all that didn't *add up to enough reasons to not do it.* We had two empty bedrooms in our house. I was home, not employed at the time. I would have the time to get him to his appointments and take care of his needs. When they heard about what we planned to do, more than one of our friends were much more uncertain. I think they were trying to protect us from more heartbreak should Oleg not be cured. Nevertheless, we made the decision to give him a home and be part of whatever was to come.

Oleg's temporary family was more than excited and extremely thankful when we called to have them return the next weekend. I spiffed up the bedroom that would become his as part of me was still saying, "What are we doing?!" Yet, there was another part that was somewhat excited to begin this chapter in our life.

Oleg arrived with everything he had in a brown grocery bag. The next day was a beautiful, warm September day. We decided to take Oleg and Oksana to visit the Mall of America. Oleg sat in the front seat, and I was seated behind him. It was warm, so Dick turned on the air conditioner with the fan on high to cool the car. From behind, I could see strands of Oleg's hair being blown out as we drove. By the next morning, clumps of his dark hair lay on his pillow. He asked Oksana to ask Dick if he would shave the rest of it off. We had thought ahead the day before and bought him a Minnesota Twins cap at the mall. It became his favorite head gear from that day forward.

Thankfully, along with Oleg came Oksana. She was such a Godsend during the first few weeks. She stayed in our home for a time and then would meet us at the hospital when Oleg was admitted for his chemo. As Oleg's English improved, they communicated mostly by phone. He was bright and eager to learn English. Almost daily, he would sit me down at the kitchen table with his Ukrainian/English dictionary. Then he would open the kitchen cabinets and refrigerator and ask, "How you say?" as he pointed to a variety of items. He was understanding us within a few weeks and speaking well enough to carry on a conversation within three or four months! He loved America, as he would often tell us, and wanted to embrace all he could as fast as possible while leaving the memories of his orphanage life behind.

Oleg was loved

I was a youth director at our church at the time, which meant Oleg was able to take part in the events we planned. I remember him coming on a retreat weekend late that fall. We awoke in the morning and didn't see him anywhere until we looked out on the lake. There he was on a paddle boat with a fishing pole in his hand...and no life jacket! The language barrier was still a challenge at that time, but somehow he understood the urgency in our voice as we requested that he come back to shore right away. Oleg loved to explore and create. I would often see his little bald head peering into a closet or drawer, looking for what he needed to make something. I would ask, "Oleg, what are you doing?" His response would often be, "You vill see" (that's not a typo). Then he would produce something like his homemade dart. It was constructed of four wooden matchsticks with a stick pin in the center, held together by wrapping thread around it, and the fins were made from paper that he had carefully folded. This dart still sits on my desk twenty-six years later. I recall why he made the dart. After one of his hospital stays, friends came by with a balloon bouquet with get well wishes imprinted on them. It was a reminder of the precious time this disease was taking from him—so he wanted a dart to pop those balloons.

When Oleg would return from his days at the hospital, his desire was to return to the life he loved as quickly as possible. He was amazing! He learned to ride a bike. One day, I wasn't sure where he had gone. Well, he knew that Dick was doing a remodel job a few blocks away, so he decided to pay him a visit. He was intrigued by all of the tools in his shop and van. Another time we wondered where he was when we saw the top of his hairless head poking around in the back of the van. He was in awe of the battery-charged tools that ran without being plugged in.... "Oh, much power!" he exclaimed.

One of his most favorite things was our trips to Walmart or as he said it "Valmart." It was like a museum for him. I could go about my shopping and return to either the fishing gear or the fish and aquarium section and there he would be, still with more he wanted to see. When his strength was up, Oleg would attend the local middle school for a half day. I would pick him up at noon. One particular day I had made a quick stop at Walmart and then picked him up. He recognized the familiar logo on the bag in the back seat and quickly asked, "You go to Valmart without me?" I had to admit to it and told him I wouldn't do it again.

Soon, a friend gave us an aquarium they no longer were using. That provided Oleg with many hours of entertainment and more opportunities for him to create something. He kept the water crystal clear, and the fish he had purchased at Valmart were beautiful.

Oleg had his first real Christmas with our family. He was so excited as he opened all his gifts and took in the festivities the holidays provided. He especially enjoyed the food. For the most part he liked whatever was on the menu, but there was something that he yearned for—bread like he ate in Ukraine. We spent time in the bakery section of several stores searching for this bread, not exactly understanding what it was we were looking for. We did know that it was a heavy, dense bread. A friend from church tried to make a few different kinds at home, to no avail. Finally, we came across a loaf of sour dough bread that passed the test. It was labeled "Nasty Bread." Of course, Oleg who was always eager to learn more English, asked the meaning of nasty. We explained it, and from then on "nasty" became part of his ever-expanding vocabulary. I recall one time as we were eating in a restaurant, we observed a boy who had yet to learn how to behave when in public. Oleg, with a serious tone said, "That is a nasty boy!"

When he was feeling well, Oleg loved to eat and even learned to do a little cooking. I remember coming home more than once to the smell of his famous fried nasty bread. We quickly opened the windows before the smoke alarm went off. The air was filled with a haze from the hot oil, and it took a couple days to rid the house of the smell. He really liked chicken and the first time I served it, I had to tell him he didn't need to eat the knuckles off the drumstick, as I passed the plate with more chicken for him to eat. Living in the orphanage, nothing went to waste, so he did not understand the concept of a garbage disposal as he saw me using it to get rid of some leftovers that had been in the refrigerator too long.

Oleg taught us so much about appreciating what we had in this country. It was the simple things that brought us all joy. If Dick and I were watching TV, sitting next to each other on the couch, Oleg would soon appear and wiggle his tiny little body right in between us. He was most content being with us and a few friends from time to time. I can still hear him laughing as he watched cartoons. One of his favorites was Garfield. He would laugh so hard at his antics that the tears would roll down his cheeks.

Oleg was wise and courageous beyond his years. He had been in the orphanage for four years after his mom died, as many others did following the Chernobyl disaster. His dad was never a part of his life. He told us about his mom walking three miles one way every day to milk cows on a dairy farm. After he was diagnosed with testicular cancer at the age of 14, he received treatment. Unfortunately, the cancer wasn't fully eradicated from his body, so a few months later it became obvious that the cancer was rearing its ugly head again. It was about then that Judy with the European Children's Fund visited the orphanage again. She was helping to facilitate adoptions with families from the U.S. On a prior visit she had met Oleg but didn't see him this time and inquired about him. In a hushed voice one of the women told her he was in a room in the back of the house. It was quite obvious to Judy that Oleg was sick. Judy knew that she needed to get him to the U.S. in hopes of him receiving the medical care he needed that could possibly save his life.

That's where we came in, along with the doctors and hospital that would soon become part of the pro-bono team, as we all cared for this young boy.

His chemotherapy to fight the rhabdomyosarcoma continued on through the fall and early winter that year. He was gaining strength and liked to be active. He raked and bagged leaves, learned to ride a bike and loved shopping, even though he never asked that we buy him anything. His friend Katie and he would go to a movie or just hang out at home. He enjoyed exploring and learning. Seeing the world through his eyes made ours so much broader and richer.

With the prescribed course of treatment at its end, surgery was scheduled for late February in hopes of getting the last bit of cancer removed. We waited in the family room at Children's Hospital in St. Paul, praying the surgeon would have good news for us. That isn't what happened. When they explored Oleg's abdominal cavity it was apparent that the cancer had metastasized—and there was nothing more they could do.

His decreasing energy and increasing discomfort became evident within a week or two. His doctor and I had discussed his prognosis and knew it was time to be honest with Oleg as to his future. I recall the day clearly. I was in the kitchen while Oleg was reclined in Dick's big chair in the living room. He called for me and asked a simple question. "No more medicine?" With a lump in my throat I responded saying, "No Oleg, there is no more medicine." The next question was just as difficult. With tears in his eyes and a tremor in his voice he said, "Then I am going to die?" I knew I had to be totally honest with him. My response was, "Oleg, unless God performs a miracle, you will die." He just sat quietly for a time and then said, "This is not fair. I lived in Ukraine and had nothing, now I am here where I have everything I could ever want and now I am going to die?!" We both cried and I agreed that it wasn't fair, but we were all going to do the best we could with whatever time he had left.

The next day Oleg shared with me that he was scared. That opened the door to conversations that soon reassured him that he need not be afraid. Since he had been part of our church and the youth group, he had heard about Jesus and His love for all of us. On our living room wall hung a framed print titled Welcome Home. It had been a gift that we received the day after Timm's death and it served as a wonderful illustration to dispel the notion that death was just a 'dark hole, lights out' as he had thought. As salvation began to settle into his heart, he seemed to accept what was coming.

There's a special story behind that Welcome Home print. Our dear friends, Marlys and Al, were at the mall the Friday night that Timm died. As they browsed through one particular store, Al was drawn to this print. It is a scene of Heaven, depicting Jesus greeting a boy as he entered. You see only the back of the boy. He had dark curly hair, just like Timm. Marlys and Al received the shocking news after they got home that night; then returned to purchase the print as soon as the mall opened the next morning. I know it took my breath away when they brought it to us. They had been admiring it the night before about the same time that Timm died. Some might call that a coincidence. I like to think of it as another "God-incidence."

Dick, Jill, Oleg and I were able to do a Make a Wish trip to Disney World. Oleg gave all he had to enjoy trading the cool damp days of early spring in Minnesota for the warm sunshine of Florida. As he sat on the edge of the bed, watching us pack up to go home that day, he said he wished we could stay in the warmth we had been enjoying for the last few days. I told him I understood and that was part of going on vacation...everyone has to go back home at some point. His response took my breath away. He looked me in the eye and quietly said, "Ok, I guess I'll go home and die then." I had no words. I gave his thin little body a hug and told him I loved him.

Jill and Oleg at Sea World

We settled back in after our trip and Oleg's health quickly deteriorated. His mind stayed alert, but his weakened body could no longer be up and around. Hospice came into play and was a wonderful support for Oleg and us as well. We had more conversations about the home he would have in Heaven when God chose to call him to come. At first, he had a hard time conceiving of a place that could be better than what he had found right here, in our home and community. Several times, as his discomfort intensified, he would say, "I am ready to go home now. Can I go home?" We would reassure Oleg that when his home was ready, he could go.

On the first day of spring in 1994 as the afternoon sun bathed his bedroom with warmth, his battle was over. It was one of the most profound and peaceful experiences of my life. As we waited for his last breath, there was a presence around me. It was as if I had Jesus on one side of me and Timm on the other, saying, "It's okay Mom, his home is ready, you can let him go."

What a privilege we had been given to be able to pour into this special boy's life for the last seven months, and then walk with him to Heaven's gates. Knowing he would meet his older brother and grand-parents there provided us with a certain peace as we released him.

For as much as people thought we did for Oleg, it was our family who received so much more. He left behind so many great memories and life lessons for us and others who got to know him. Though it may sound strange to some, I would do it all over again, even knowing the same outcome.

I believe that as always, God had a plan. I was unable to be with Timm when he died, so God gave us this special child who so needed to be loved and cared for, even as he died.

Chapter 11

The United Nation Comes to Hastings

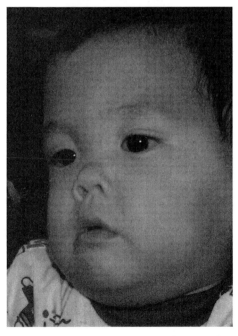

The first photo we saw of Brandon

Donna Mathiowetz ❖ 73

Springtime brings new life and changes, especially when you live in Minnesota. But, for us spring brought changes that no one could have predicted. Timm died in March, as did Oleg, two years apart. "Our plan" was still to adopt a baby or two. How very different the Master's Plan can be! In January of 1995, our friends told us about a two-year-old boy in Hawaii. Their friends attended the same church as the boy's foster parents. They were a military family and had decided that, given Brandon would need ongoing therapy and medical support due to his cerebral palsy, he would need a more stable home, as military transfers were very common. Brandon was born at twenty-five weeks, weighing only one pound-thirteen ounces. Of course, he was physically delayed and his prognosis wasn't yet clear.

Our friends contemplated and prayed about it and decided adoption wasn't for them, but they knew we were in the process of doing just that. Again, Dick and I looked at each other and wondered if this was the direction we were to go. We had several conversations with Diane, Brandon's foster mom, along with a picture that was faxed to us. Brandon was an adorable little guy (weighing in at twenty pounds at two years old) with dark almond eyes and black hair. He actually looked a lot like me. Was it a coincidence that I had often been asked if I was of Asian descent? No, I'm Norwegian and Finnish.

Yet another surprise presented itself while were working out some details in Hawaii. Literally out of the blue, we were contacted by an agency in Iowa that was facilitating adoptions out of a Russian orphanage. There was an eleven-year-old girl with a heart and lung condition. They wanted to bring her to the U.S. for treatment and were in need of a family. To this day, we aren't sure of how they got our name, but God knows. Again, if this was to be, the pieces of the puzzle would need to fit together.

We hadn't budgeted for a winter vacation that year, but we so wanted to meet Brandon in person. God had that all figured out as well. I found round trip flights that we could afford, and a gracious family from his church offered us their extra bedroom with a walkout that led to the beach just two blocks away. We arrived in time to celebrate Brandon's second birthday, on March 20, 1995. As we took our morning walks along the beautiful beach, I remember talking and praying about Svetlana, the little Russian girl in need of a home and foster family. We returned home assured that things would be happening, not knowing how or when. Well, just in time for Easter, Svetlana arrived, and with her, new challenges. A new home, culture, and language made life a bit chaotic for everyone. I compared it to being dropped onto another planet.

Then, on Memorial Day weekend, Brandon and his foster mom Diane, arrived from Hawaii. She returned home after a week with us and Brandon was ours. So, two children were added to our family within a month of each other, both requiring a lot of love and a lot of energy. Brandon's adoption was finalized a year later, and Svetlana was eventually adopted by another family. Today, she is married and doing well, and still living in the U.S.

Well, spring arrived again the next year. This time the call came from an agency in Indianapolis. They were bringing children to the U.S. who were in need of medical treatment which was unavailable in their own country. Sahr was a six-year-old boy from Sierra Leone, Africa. He had what they called wind swept deformity or sometimes called Z legs. Both his legs were swayed to one side and back again. If not corrected, the weight of his body as he grew would render him unable to stand or walk. Sahr would require surgery at a hospital in Minneapolis, so I flew to Indiana and returned with him. His new brother and sister were eagerly waiting to meet him. The empty bedrooms in our house were no longer empty, that's for sure. Sahr was with us for six months and then adopted by another family in rural Minnesota.

The next April another organization reached out to us. Do you see a pattern here? They also brought children to the U.S. in need of medical care. Our next surprise was Lydia, a two-year-old beautiful little girl from the Dominican Republic. She would need two surgeries to correct a birth defect, that if not corrected, would cause her to be ostracized in her community as well as putting her at great risk for infections. Her parents entrusted her first to a flight attendant who was her escort as she made her way here on a late-night flight. She was handed over to us, looking wide eyed and bewildered by it all. Again, like Oleg and Svetlana, our language was not hers. Brandon and she became fast friends. Even though they were two years apart in age, they were similar in size.

At birth, Lydia needed a stoma, which involved a procedure to place two small holes in her side to allow for the drainage of waste. Unfortunately, in her home country, there was no access to colostomy bags, so instead she was wrapped in a cloth which was changed as it became saturated. Needless to say, I had to take a crash course in how to take care of this need. It was not something I had planned on learning, but these types of things had become a way of life for us. With all the children's various doctor appointments and hospital stays over the previous four years, I was often asked if I was a nurse. No, not by book-smart standards, but life lessons and immersion instead.

Lydia became such a special addition to our family. She adjusted well and Brandon and she became very close. Needless to say, she brought us a lot of joy. Lydia required two surgeries. One to open her anus and a few months later a second surgery to redirect her digestive tract to the right place and suture the two small holes in her side. Once those were completed, it was time to start planning for her trip home where her anxious family was waiting. There had been only minimal communication with them, and that was through the doctor in the Dominican Republic who spoke English. Lydia, now almost three years old, would be returning home to her Spanish speaking family with English now being her first language. We knew this would be a traumatic transition for her as we had become the only family she knew.

Lydia added so much to our family in the eleven months she was with us, and we knew she would be greatly missed. Brandon and she had become so close, that where you saw one, you saw the other. Lydia mimicked anything she observed Brandon doing. She wasn't sucking her thumb until she saw Brandon doing it. What she didn't understand was that it was also necessary to swallow from time to time. It wasn't unusual to see saliva running down her arm.

We booked our flight to bring her home and made reservations to stay at a resort to have a few days of vacation before returning to Minnesota. On the second day there, we had arranged for Lydia's family to come to the hotel to get her. Dick went to the front desk that morning to inquire about something and noticed a couple with two children sitting on a sofa in the lobby area. He surmised that it was Lydia's family. He walked over and asked, "Lydia?" With that, they all four sprang from their seats and said "se!" With a hand motion, he told them to wait a minute and he came back to our room. Our emotions went to a whole new level, while little Lydia had no idea what was about to happen. She was dressed in one of her many darling outfits, her beautiful brown skin was glowing and her curly hair smelled of baby shampoo. It was time. The next few minutes were as a scene from a movie. As soon as we emerged from the hallway, her mother came running, eager to hold her baby who she hadn't seen in almost a year. Lydia tightened her grasp around my neck and held her legs firmly around my waist. Her mother then lifted her dress to see that the holes in her side were no more. Understandably, few words were exchanged, just a lot of smiles and tears.

Her family was grateful and wanted to do something for us. With the help of a hotel employee interpreting, they invited us to go home with them so we could see where they lived. What could we say? We all piled into their small car and off we went. That became one of those rides you don't forget. Let's say traffic laws are sparse, if any! I did some extra praying and was relieved when we arrived at their pallet-and-dirt-floor home. The neighbors were all around and cheering as Lydia exited the car, however she was not impressed.

We unpacked the collection of clothing Lydia had acquired from so many generous friends and family while she was with us. I had put together a photo album filled with happy times and good memories that we shared with her family. Lydia stayed close to my side, not open to her family's desire to engage her. They insisted that we return later in the week to have dinner and arranged a time to pick us up. Then it was time to go back to the hotel...more prayers! Prayers for travel, but also for Lydia. She really didn't want us to leave her in this place—where she didn't ever remember being. Peeling her out of my arms was gut-wrenching for her and for us as well.

We returned later in the week so they could express their gratitude one more time and we could say our final goodbye to Lydia. It was very sweet. They had prepared what would be considered an elaborate meal for them. There was roasted chicken that had probably just been running through the house a few hours earlier before it succumbed to the chopping block out back. The salad was green and leafy with other veggies mixed in. The juice was fruity. I remember a white tablecloth with a few flowers in a glass of water as a centerpiece. We ate as the whole family stood and watched, insisting that we eat more. The happiness in that home was palpable. Their baby was home and healthy...not yet happy, but that would come. We flew back home the next day. After that special meal, served with so much love and gratitude, let's just say we were glad to be close to the bathroom on the plane.

People often ask if we have been in touch with Lydia's family. No, we haven't. It's a third-world country. God willing, we would love to go there some day and maybe with a miracle, we could see that little girl who now is a young woman, most likely with a family of her own.

Chapter 12

Brandon's Extended Hospital Stay

A sunny day at Children's Hospital

November 1997

For the most part, life was humming along and excitement was building as the three kids were anticipating Thanksgiving and Christmas.. We were also planning our twenty-fifth wedding anniversary where we would renew our vows, celebrating with family and friends. Brandon, our then four-year-old adopted son, was scheduled for a shunt revision, as we had detected a small blockage in the mechanism. It was expected to be a same-day surgery. At this point Lydia was still with us, waiting for the second of her two surgeries.

I clearly recall that Sunday in November. Dick, Svetlana, Brandon, Lydia, and I had returned from church, and as I was preparing lunch, I heard a strange noise from the garage below. I sensed that it was something I should check out. As I opened the door that led out to the garage, I saw Dick lying on the floor. He was fully conscious, but as I looked down at his leg it was obvious that it was broken. He had been using a ladder to go up into a space above the garage. When he placed his foot on the step of the ladder to come down, the ladder slid out from under him. He fell ten feet onto the concrete floor. He hadn't hit his head or hurt his back, thankfully. Dick was and still is a self-employed contractor/remodeler.

In all honesty, one of the first thoughts that came to me as I knelt over him was, how are we going to support this family? We didn't have any employees who would show up tomorrow morning to keep the income coming in. My mind briefly began to race as I thought of the three kids in the house. How would we mange without an income? God quickly brought me back to the immediate issue at hand. I called 911 and then prayed over Dick. My next call was to our friend Pam, asking her to come ASAP to take care of the kids who were fourteen, four, and two and unaware of what had just happened. We waited for the ambulance and after ten minutes, Dick said he thought he could get into the van so I could drive him to our local hospital. By the grace of God, we managed that. I told the kids that Pam would be there in a few minutes and off we went. Dick had surgery that afternoon and came home the next day, cast, crutches and all.

Everyone is going to have seasons in their lives which we can't handle on our own. We found ourselves now in one of those times. As scheduled, four days after Dick broke his leg, Brandon and I went to his appointment at Children's Hospital in St. Paul. The procedure which was supposed to be a same-day experience turned into ten days in the Pediatric Intensive Care Unit (PICU). The attempt to replace the mechanism resulted in a bleed to the brain followed by two more surgeries and multiple tense moments covered in a lot of prayer. Dick made his way to the hospital almost every day, learning how to maneuver with crutches and a wheelchair. I never left the hospital, relying on people to bring me what I needed from home. Many of those same people were the ones helping to maintain some normalcy for our two kids at home and keeping the prayer teams informed with updates on Brandon. Our daughter Jill was away at college and came home often to do what she could.

Word spread quickly through our community and people earnestly wanted to know what they could do to help. These were people not just from our own church family, but several others as well. Having a place for Svetlana and Lydia was our first concern and that was resolved quickly. Next on my list was the financial needs. Making sure we could pay our insurance premium was paramount. When Marty, a friend from a neighboring church called to ask how they could help, I shared that need with her. She asked how much it was. The cost of insurance when you're self-employed is hefty. We would need $500. Without hesitation, Marty replied, "We will have that for you this week."

I had mailed the invitations for our anniversary celebration before all of these unforeseen events had happened. With the love and efforts of many friends and family, we did celebrate. The very best part was that the morning of the party, Brandon was released from PICU and moved to a regular room. His PCA (personal care assistant) Jill, came to sit with him, and I was able to go home and attend the party. We felt the love and support from so many that afternoon. I returned to the hospital in the evening, and the next day Brandon was released to come home. We were exhausted, but everyone was back together. Over the next weeks and months, there were appointments with doctors and therapists. Even though there were several times during his hospital stay when no one was certain how this was going to end, Brandon rallied and returned to good health.

Four days after getting home was Thanksgiving and we certainly had much for which to be thankful. God's provision continued to pour into our lives. Dick wasn't able to return to work until early January. How did a family of five survive without an income for almost two months? We did more than survive. We were blessed in so many ways. Just prior to all of this, we felt we were supposed to make some changes, which included finding a new church. We had been visiting a couple churches, discerning which one we would call "home". The church we would be leaving graciously hosted our anniversary party and collected a special Sunday morning offering for us. Another church started a food train. The afternoon we brought Brandon home, the smell of lasagna in the oven greeted us—and they had cleaned the house too. They also put up the Christmas tree, decorated in part with twenty-dollar bills clipped on with clothespins. There were countless others who were going to make sure our Thanksgiving meal lacked nothing. On more than one occasion, I would go to answer the door to find no one there except for the turkey and fixings left on the front step. In fact, we didn't have room for all the food so we were able to donate a nice package to our local food shelf to bless someone else. People randomly stopped by, handing us a check or cash wrapped in a hug and a prayer.

Our kids were showered with plenty of Christmas gifts under the tree, more than if we would have done the shopping, for sure. As we turned the calendar page to 1998, we were current with all our bills and had more in the checking account than we did two months earlier. Beyond being covered with the financial blessings was knowing that we were part of a community of people who truly cared for us.

Dig your well before you get thirsty.
When we are faithful in caring for others,
we in turn will be loved and cared for as well.

What we experienced was nothing short of miraculous. How did this all happen? I believe it goes back to that well from which we were able to draw water. The law of reciprocity is proven to be real.

- What we sow into the lives of others will be returned into our lives.
- The help we received wasn't determined by where we attended church every Sunday morning.
- We were just one of the families who needed some help.
- We had been there for people in the past in different times of need.

- Each time we help one another, our own well goes a little deeper, tapping into the waters of grace and mercy for others.
- We reap what we sow.

Celebrating Jill's college graduation

Brandon at his place

Part III

Time Marches On...Entering the New Season

Chapter 13

The Empty Nest

2019

❝ Life goes on." I remember more than one person saying that to me in the months and years after Timm's and Oleg's deaths. It didn't sit well with me then. It was painfully obvious that life had seemed to certainly move on for almost everyone around me.

The good news is that years later my life was able to go on as well, just not as quickly as some would hope or expect.

Jill, Al, Emma, Ean, Ellie, and Hank

Our daughter Jill is married to Al, and they blessed us with three of the best and brightest grandchildren anyone could have. They live just thirty minutes away. Emma, Ean and Ellie all play hockey, and we do our best to keep up with their schedules. We share stories of Timm, Oleg and the other kids our grandchildren never got to meet.

Brandon was able to move into his own apartment in a nearby city. With the help of some support staff for cooking, cleaning, and shopping, he is doing well. He is employed and enjoys life. When we adopted Brandon and his special needs, we knew early on that he someday would live outside of our home. For us, the plan was never to have him live at home until our own age or health no longer allowed it. It took a lot of time and energy to find the right place for him to live and work. Seeing that plan now a reality gives us peace. There are always some bumps on the road, but we all continue to learn as we go.

We were fortunate to have a large enough home for our expanding family at the time. A lot of great memories have been created in that home, along with others that are precious, though sad. Dick's dad spent a short time in hospice care in a bed set up in our living room, and died there with some of his family close by.

Oleg lived a brief life there that he had only dreamed of and was able to go right from the comfort of his bedroom to Heaven's gates.

Brandon came to that home as a little guy to become our "forever boy," as he used to say. He recuperated from three surgeries in the hospital bed set up in the downstairs family room.

Our three foster children, Svetlana, Sahr, and Lydia each added their own stories to our home as only they could.

Some days were so exhausting, but the memories we have and what we learned from each of them, are priceless.

The wonderful home that for a time had been filled with joy and activity now found Dick and me occupying less than half of the available space. We realized it was time to take the big step to downsize and simplify. I had been ready to do this for a couple of years, but had to wait patiently (most of the time) for Dick to arrive at the same place in his heart and mind. It wasn't just about the house. He also would be giving up a pretty sweet heated garage and shop which some referred to as the "Garage Mahal."

The weekend before we were scheduled to sign the papers and officially list the property, I felt some apprehension about moving forward with our plans. That Sunday morning, as I was having my quiet time, I checked in with God to ask if this was the right time. All I heard was, "Throw out the fleece." It truly came out of the blue as it had nothing to do with my Bible reading that day. I recalled the story in the book of Judges where Gideon tested God with a wool fleece. What else could that message mean? Opening my Bible, I turned to Judges 6:36–40 to refresh my mind with the story. A peace came over me, and I truly felt that God was directing us to move forward. I shared it with Dick—and we took the next steps with even more trust in God's plan for our future.

Happy Grandma

This is us in 2019

Chapter 14

Bittersweet Memories

O ur house was homey and spacious and had lots of storage space. What do most people do with lots of storage space over twenty-six years of time? Collect stuff! To prepare to put the house on the market, we began to clean out, sell, donate, and toss. It is a lot of work, but it feels so good. Well, to be honest, some parts didn't feel all that good. For the last twenty-six years in the back of the family room closet were two large bags that had traveled with us through two moves. Every now and then, Dick would say, "We need to go through those one of these days." Those white-handled bags with the swirly blue graphics held all the sympathy and thinking-of-you cards and letters we had received in the months after Timm's death.

Dick was determined to look at each one. For me, it didn't seem necessary. Again, we each needed to do what was best for us, individually. He did set aside a pile of special cards and letters from those closest to

Timm or to us, as well as those who were complete strangers who had also lost a child. These writers shared in their own words how deeply they had been affected by this tragedy. Some took the time to recall a memory of Timm as a little boy, like the woman who shared the story of Timm at her son's seventh birthday party. She could still see him sitting on the front step, eating an orange Popsicle, seeing it dripping off his elbow. Another told us how much her son had looked up to Timm. He had intervened when her son was being bullied by someone at school. A former librarian remembered him as a cute little boy, always friendly with a sparkle in his eyes.

Several of these messages came months and even years later...
it really is never too late for an act of compassion and kindness.

Then we came across boxes and bins of pictures. If you are older than fifty you most likely can relate. We used to print pictures (and usually doubles which I intended to share, but most often never did). Along with that, as our parents and other relatives died, we acquired the pictures we had given to them. By now, we may have four or five copies of the same print. You get the "picture." During an early spring snowstorm the year we moved, we began the task of sorting through them. We made it through two or three boxes before I was exhausted. The memories of days gone by as I saw that handsome little dark-haired boy over and over were really hard. Plus, we had all the images of other loved ones who were gone as well.

Danny and me

After Timm and Oleg, we grieved the deaths of our four parents, two brothers-in-law, two nephews and some close life-long friends. These were more bitter-sweet memories of what our family used to be, all there in those boxes and bins. I knew it was a job that needed to be done. Our next home would not have the space to store them. Every week or two, we would take a deep breath, and commit to this task for an hour or two at a time. The old adage rang true, "How do you eat an elephant? One bite at a time!"

Timm was athletic and a good hockey player. I recall him pushing a chair around the arena as he was learning to skate as a first grader. He played left wing and scored his share of the goals. Along with all the pictures we had, his big gold hockey bag had already traveled to our various homes. It found its place under the stairs of our split-entry home. Every year or two we would clean out under those stairs, disturbing a few spiders along the way. The bag remained tucked away in the far corner for years.

I mentioned earlier that our three grandkids all play hockey. Our daughter Jill decided to redo their downstairs family room and chose a hockey theme. She asked if she could have the big gold bag. We were happy that she felt ready to have it, and now their family room displays a couple classic sticks, Timm's jersey, gloves, and even a pair of skates. We're grateful they all have found a home—and are another way to keep Timm's memory alive.

If you talk to anyone who has endured a traumatic loss,
they most likely will use the term "triggers."
These are those seemingly little things that catch us off guard,
sending a wave of emotion for which we weren't prepared.

One of what seems like thousands of these times happened to me just a couple years ago. I had taken my grandson, Ean, to a local school to get his team and individual hockey pictures taken. He was all suited up and just needed help with tying his skates. I knelt down in front of him. This very vivid memory rushed over me as I recalled doing the same thing for Timm so many times. I wanted to be able to raise my head, look up and see Timm sitting on that bench in front of me.

Our granddaughter Emma's team plays games in our town of Hastings. Years ago, the local arena added an additional sheet of indoor ice along with the original one our kids had played on years ago. I had not been back in that building since Timm played his last game just a month before he died. The first time I sat in those bleachers, watching her play on the same ice as Timm had was tough. I could so easily visualize Timm doing the same and see him sitting out his two-minute penalty in the box across from where I was seated. I still have a few of those flashbacks when I watch Emma play, but it no longer takes my breath away.

I know that if you've suffered a significant loss, you will relate to the bittersweet memories. Until the local Burger King remodeled its restaurant years after Timm's death, whenever Dick and I went there, I would look at the table Timm and I sat at the night before he died. I also remember having a difficult time when we traded the car we had when he died. My heart knew that he used to ride in that car, and that he would never occupy the new minivan in the garage.

So many memories. One of Timm's admirable qualities was his ability to connect with people. Just a couple weeks before he died, Timm had gone to Minneapolis with us to serve lunch at a homeless shelter. At one point I didn't see him in the dining area. Then I spotted him off in the corner engaged in a conversation with one of the men who had come for lunch. He seemed comfortable with pretty much anyone. He loved babies, even tiny babies. Timm was also attentive to his aging grandparents too. I'm sure his great people skills would have been an asset in his adult life. I recall one of his teachers telling me, "I know that if Timm would have had the chance to grow up, he would have been a fine man." The phrase, "I wonder what Timm would be...?" still crosses our minds and sometimes our lips.

The Soul Grows Through Suffering

Jonathon Edwards, in a famous sermon on the book of Job, noted that the story of Job is the story of us all. Job lost everything in one day: his family, his wealth, and his health. Most of us experience our losses more slowly—over the span of a lifetime—until we find ourselves on the door of death, leaving everything behind.

Catastrophic loss by definition precludes recovery. It will transform us or destroy us, but it will never leave us the same. There is no going back to the past.

It is not therefore true that we become less through loss—unless we allow the loss to make us less, grinding our soul down until there is nothing left.

Loss can make us more.

I did not get over the loss of my loved ones; rather, I absorbed the loss into my life, until it became part of who I am.

Sorrow took up permanent residence in my soul and enlarged it.

One learns the pain of others by suffering one's own pain, by turning inside oneself, by finding one's own soul.

However painful, sorrow is good for the soul.

The soul is elastic, like a balloon.

It can grow larger through suffering.

Used with permission
Jerry Sittser is an author and theologian whose wife, daughter, and mother all died in a tragic car accident.

Part IV

Come Alongside

Chapter 15

Come Alongside

—You Have So Much to Offer, and They Need You

Just because I carry it well doesn't mean it isn't heavy.
— Bill Bennot

My belief is that those of us who have not just survived but are actually thriving after the loss of a loved one, have a responsibility to educate others. How else will they understand? Quite often within our grief group we joke about being able to write a book on *all the things not to say to a grieving person*. I remind them that I believe ninety-nine percent of those who have hurt us or have been less than helpful acted out of ignorance. All of us feel as if we need to say something in those awkward and uncomfortable moments. What is true is that often, the less said, the better. Maybe that's why God gave us two ears and one mouth.

I believe that God's design is one of people being there for each other in all circumstances. We are eager to celebrate the happy times such as weddings, graduations, and the birth of new baby.

What we need to improve is how we come alongside others as the circle of life here on earth is completed.

I truly appreciate and admire those who will come to a grief group with the grieving person. All have shared that they were able to learn things they had not known before. I am often asked, "I want to be there for my friend but how can I help?" My advice is that if possible, coming with them to a group would be a wonderful gift. It takes courage to walk through the doors to become a member of a club *you never wanted to join*. Having someone else to lean on can mean the world to the one carrying the heavy load of loss and grief. Many of those who have been there as support are exceedingly grateful, and actually are also surprised by how much more they now understand.

I'd like to share some other very practical ways to sincerely help. Keep in mind the one mouth and two ears that we're each given. Above all other suggestions is that we should all be quicker to listen and slower to speak.

❖

Be quick to listen, slow to speak and slow to get angry.
— James 1:19

The person in pain, most of all, may need to talk and have someone who is willing to listen with their heart. I remember someone telling me that I should tell my story...until I grew tired of hearing it. Well, here I am almost thirty years later, still telling my story. You may hear them retell the story of the death over and over again. Listen attentively each time. Realize that repetition is part of your friend's healing process. Simply listen. What you and I both know is that we don't have any magic words to offer to the grieving when the only thing that would relieve their pain is for their loved one to walk back through the door. Think about coming alongside to be someone who "walks with," not "behind" or "in front of" the one who is bereaved.

Avoid the clichés that are trite comments often intended to diminish the loss by providing simple solutions to difficult realities. Comments such as, "You are holding up so well," "Time will heal all wounds," "Think of all you have to be thankful for," or "Just be happy that he's out of his pain," are not constructive. Instead, they hurt and make a friend's journey through grief even more painful. Please avoid using the term *"at least..."* These are words that will rarely be helpful and almost always hurtful. When we use these words, we immediately minimize the pain the grieving person is experiencing. It conveys to them that maybe they shouldn't feel so bad...because it could be worse. It may make them hesitant to be open about how they're feeling when what they need is to be able to talk to someone who can just listen.

It's also important to remember that the *experience of loss and grief is not meant to be a competition of whose pain was greater.* If your purpose is to be there as a support for someone who is grieving, do your best not to interject your own story of loss unless they ask you to share it. It's not about whose loss was greater. Bring the conversation back to them and just listen or be still with them.

Those of us who have walked the path of grief often hear people say, "Call me if there's anything you need." I know this is a well-intended and sincere offer. However, it is highly unlikely that we would be the ones to ask for help. I remember not even understanding what people thought I might need. You see, during the early days, weeks and months, when you are buried in the pain of grief, a small victory will be getting out of bed, brushing your teeth, and accomplishing the bare minimum that the day will require. That is why we need a brave soul or two to come to us— and just do what we can't. In the deepest and most painful times of the journey, the only thing that could help is for our loved one to walk back through the door.

Understand that everyone's grief experience is unique. No one will respond to the death of someone they loved in exactly the same way. While it may be possible to talk about similar phases shared by grieving people, everyone is different and shaped by experiences in his or her life. The relationship that one person had with the deceased may be very different than the other. For some, woven in with the grief of death may be the grief for what never was.

It's important to be patient as the process can take a long time. There is no timetable. By walking with your loved one in grief, you are giving one of life's most important gifts: yourself and your time without expectations.

Offer practical help such as preparing food, washing clothes, cleaning the house, mowing the lawn, shoveling snow or other practical ways of showing that you care. These things are needed not only in the immediate days surrounding the death, but also in the weeks and months to come. Remain available long after the flurry of activities have ended. I remember the utter emptiness I felt as everyone around me got back to life—and I wondered how I was going to survive.

Of course, there are times when you need to say something or write it in a card or text. There really is no substitute for your personal written words. Share a favorite story about the person who died. Relate the special qualities you remember about him or her. These words will often be a loving gift to your grieving friend; words that will be reread and remembered for years. Please use the name of the person who has died either in your personal note or when you talk to your friend. Hearing their name is like music to their ears. It is comforting, and it confirms that you have not forgotten this important person who was so much a part of their lives. I've heard people say that they hesitate to say the deceased person's name for fear that it may make the grieving person sad and cry. What I know is that the sadness and tears are right under the surface anyway. You have just given them permission to let them out.

I read something written by Terry Kettering a while back that I think captures this concept so well. The author talked about "the elephant in the room; that being the unspoken truth that someone had died, and yet no one seemed to want to speak of him or her. The trivial niceties being spoken were deafening to the person feeling totally alone in a roomful of people. The grieving person wants to shout, "Please say their name, please say it again...otherwise I am going to be left alone in this room with this elephant."

Sensitive Support
Here are a few more practical ways to be supportive.

Helpful words:
- I'm sorry for your loss.
- I miss her too; can I share a story with you?

- We'll take care of keeping your sidewalk shoveled/grass cut.
- I'm going to the store, is there anything you need?
- We're going to the park. Can we pick up your kids and take them too?
- I can't understand your pain, but just know I'm here for you.
- This is going to take time, please be kind to yourself.
- We don't have to talk; I'll just sit with you for a while.
- Can I do your laundry/clean your house?

Hurtful Words:
- At least he's out of his pain and in a better place.
- You're young, you can find love again.
- You're young; you can have another child.
- Hang in there, you're strong.
- I know exactly how you feel.
- Well, let me tell you what happened to me.
- Be grateful you still have three other children.
- Maybe you just need to _____.
- It's been a year now...it must be getting better.
- I guess God needed her.

You can probably add a few more do's and don'ts to what I've shared. Grief is a mysterious beast, and there is no perfect way to go through it. Say "something," because the opposite is perceived as not caring. Just remember, less over the long haul, is more.

I believe the best teachers are those who are on the journey of grief themselves. Anyone who has suffered a loss knows that journey continues, to some degree, through the rest of our lives. I reached out to a few of the people I have had the privilege of getting to know over the last few years. These precious souls have been through the hardest times of their lives. They are all at different junctures on their own journey of grief. Some would say there are days when they feel as if they are just surviving—and some have healed to a point of thriving, having adapted and accepted life as it is without their loved one. Any healing they have gained wasn't done in a vacuum. There were people in their lives who weren't afraid to step up and help.

A few of them graciously agreed to contribute to the Come Alongside chapter in the book so I asked them to consider three questions:

1. What have others said or done that you found to be helpful?
2. On the other hand, what wasn't helpful and possibly hurtful?
3. Have you come to a place in your grief journey where you can recognize meaning, purpose, or hope within the loss? This often can take years to uncover.

Here's some of what they thoughtfully shared with me.

Mike and Patty's son John died unexpectedly in November 2017 at the age of thirty-two.

After the loss of our son John, we found ourselves on the receiving end of much love and attention. We were overwhelmed by friends, family, neighbors, and people *we didn't even know*. Our hearts were humbled and blessed!

What we found to be most helpful was when a friend or family member would spend time with us and just listen—when we were allowed to talk and feel what we were feeling, and say what was on our hearts. Nothing more was needed. Please just visit with that grieving loved one. *They aren't going to call you when they need to talk!*

After our grief settled, we found a grief support group that was specifically for grieving parents. This provided us with emotional support and it also gave our lives a sense of normalcy. We felt a kinship with complete strangers. We found a safe place where our grief was understood and validated, as only another grieving parent could give us.

On the other hand, what was unhelpful was when some of our closest and dearest humans *unknowingly added to our pain*. The desire of their hearts was to fix and help us heal. Their well-intended, heartfelt words were what we found to be the least helpful thing you can do for your loved one. Telling me that "God was merciful in taking our son home" or "John has fulfilled his mission on earth" or "Death is just a veil," etc. These words sound good to those delivering the words, but to the grieving mom it sounds like I shouldn't feel the way I do. *It makes me feel as though my grief isn't valid.* Please do not tell your bereaved loved one how they should feel. Don't try to fix them with kind, well-meaning words. Simply be there for them. Show up.

At this time on her journey, Patty says she has not yet found meaning in losing John. "I feel like I'm just now coming out of the grief fog. The pain is not as intense, and I am able to look back over the past two-and-a-half years and say that I've come a long way. This gives me hope."

Michelle's seventeen-year-old son Joe died by suicide in June 2019.

I believe the most helpful thing for me has been the Gone Too Soon grief group. Being with other parents who understand my pain has meant so much to me. Some have taken me under their wing and loved me as their own. In addition to that group, has been an amazing supportive family, community, and school. My co-workers have helped me in many ways. Our church family has provided what we have needed at the right time. People haven't been afraid to admit that they feel helpless and really want to know what they can do to help.

The difficult times have been numerous. Watching Joe's friends' lives move on, as they should, has been painful. I so wanted to see Joe going on to school after graduation, along with his friends. I'm happy for their achievements, bittersweet as they are.

My meaning in life stems from a desire to live a life that would make Joe proud of me. He has two little sisters that need me to give whatever I am able to do each day to build a future us. Who Joe was in life gives me strength.

Our nephew Christopher died by suicide at the age of 21 in November 2010.

His mom, Jeanne shared this.

For the first days and weeks after Chris' death, a few friends came over and just sat with me. There wasn't much to say, and this meant so much to me. Then I spent more time alone in my grief.

I began sensing Chris' presence at 3:30 a.m. every morning. Even my dog would wake up and bark. I decided to invite a priest over to pray a blessing on me and my home. A new friend I had met at church during the Christmas season was there as well. She invited me to join her for Christmas Day, which was such a painful time. My sister Jacque and her husband Wayne were faithful with their calls as they just listened and let me cry. Kelly, Chris' boss and mentor at Pioneer Sand, where he worked was a tremendous help as well. When I would stop by, he'd share stories about Chris and give me a hug.

Friends had left several little one-sentence notes at Chris' memorial. It was helpful to me to read them; some even made me laugh. It seems I learned more about who Chris was through those notes.

After a while, I realized I needed to speak of Chris' suicide in order to heal, and I began telling some of my trusted clients and close friends. I felt supported with lots of hugs and tears, and it really did help.

Willie died of COPD at the age of 81 in December 2017.

Joann, his wife of 18 years, shared her reflections.

As I was recalling what seemed most helpful to me during the most difficult time of my grief, these things came to mind.

Someone inviting me to a movie...maybe a good comedy. I have never liked doing that alone.

Along those same lines, I appreciated being asked to go out to eat or being invited to their home for a meal, and then enjoying the leftovers they sent home with me. Cooking for one was difficult.

I liked being included in a project at church or in the community as it helped me think of someone other than myself.

Having those around me who were willing to just listen, without expectations or pressure, was always welcomed.

Sometimes I would hear things that though were not intended to be unhelpful, at least that is how I perceived them. Hearing, "You look so good!" on the day of Willie's funeral induced instant guilt on my part. Also, feeling pressured when asked, "How are you REALLY doing?" as if I had lied the first time she asked.

Any meaning that has come since his death is surely an ongoing process. I surprised myself at how dependent I had become. That's not necessarily a bad thing, but I was just more familiar with being completed/complemented by another person. Spiritually speaking, I believe God has a plan for me even—or maybe especially as a single person.

Camille's husband Kirk died in March 2016 of cancer. They had been married for 29 years.

Camille reflected about the many ways that people were supportive and helpful to her, stating that the many kindnesses shown to her family will never be forgotten:

- Phone calls to check in that included asking me questions and allowing me to talk.
- Texts letting me know they were thinking of me and praying for me.
- Being intentional about inviting me out for my birthday.
- Neighbors seeing me struggle and jumping in to help.
- Lawn mowing...snow shoveling...caring for my dog.
- Notes and cards, especially on special days like the anniversary of the day I lost him.
- People sharing stories about Kirk, telling me they loved and missed him too.
- People who sent me pictures of him.
- Coworkers taking tasks off my plate.
- Being part of the grief group and some members reaching out to me.
- My own reading and research on grief.

She added it helped her to:
Work out physically
Volunteer and help others

She also had a shorter list of *what didn't help*:

- People who didn't listen.
- Those who would use the knowledge of my experience to talk about their loss, but not giving me a chance to share my own loss.
- Ignoring or avoiding me.
- The insensitivity of those who would speak negatively about their own husbands when I had just lost mine.
- Being told they would invite me to dinner, etc., and then not follow through.
- Those that didn't accept my choice to date and marry again.

Have you found a meaning in light of Kirk's death?

- I have found meaning in that I can name some ways that losing Kirk has matured me.
- I am closer to my kids—and them to me.
- I treasure the goodness in life and the ability to feel joy.
- I know what's important, and don't let little things bother me.
- I live my life to the fullest knowing things can change in an instant.
- I love with no holds barred.
- I know that I have something special to offer others who go through this.

But I will never just accept that his death had to happen. After much soul searching, I see his death/cancer/painful struggles as a symptom of a fallen world—and I give thanks that I will see him again someday in heaven.

Treya delivered her stillborn baby, Ada Jean, just a few months ago.

I asked Treya what was helpful.
Honestly, after the loss of a stillborn baby, I didn't know what I needed. And those around me who knew what had happened, which was a very small circle at first, really didn't know what to do or say. But any type of effort to show us they loved us and cared meant the world. Sending flowers, meals, and cards... letting us know we were being thought of and prayed for was the most comforting. A simple "we love you and we are so sorry" is what we needed most.

Then I asked what was not helpful.
Because stillborn death is the kind of topic that people don't freely speak about, a lot of people paired it with miscarriage, because I think miscarriage is more talked about. Therefore, I got a lot of people who had experienced a miscarriage say things like "We went

through this same thing" or "I know exactly how you feel."

And as much as I know people were trying to be helpful, I didn't like that. It made me angry in some ways. My heart breaks for those who have experienced miscarriage—and the loss of a child is horrific at any stage of pregnancy or life. But being told that others "knew exactly how I felt" was not helpful. If you know someone who is grieving, I suggest instead you say, "I have no idea how you're feeling or how hard this must be, but I'm praying for you." Or if you have experienced loss and want the person to know you can understand on some level, say something like "having experienced loss myself, my heart truly goes out to you." Don't ever tell someone you know exactly how they feel—because even if you had also experienced the same type of loss, everyone's grief journey and feelings throughout it are different.

Brenden was 19 when he died by suicide in March 2015

His mom, Tammy, thought about the three questions and shared this.

What have others said or done that you found to be helpful?

The biggest thing in the beginning was to be present. They listened to me cry as I tried to make sense of something that just didn't make sense! I really appreciated those people who came and didn't try to "fix" me or offer a ton of advice. They listened or just sat quietly with me or watched TV with me.

Another thing I found really helpful were the people who didn't ask me what I needed, or how they could help, but just took initiative to do something for us. Some dropped off meals and offered to help with dishes or laundry.

I really appreciated when people shared stories of Brenden. They expressed the love they had for my son, the things Brenden did to help them, or just funny experiences they shared together. It helped me keep his memory alive! What a blessing it is to have people remember him, talk about him and share those things with me!

The last thing, but definitely not the least is the prayers people offered for me and my family. When a child dies by suicide the stigma is real. The people who said they believed Brenden was in Heaven, and that they would pray for us to have strength to cope, strength to survive, and to have peace that Brenden was indeed in heaven, was a huge comfort and support.

On the other hand, what wasn't helpful?

It's hard because most of the time I knew people were saying things out of love and a desire to help, but sometimes it did not. People said things like, this was

God's plan, that Brenden was now an angel in God's army or that he was "in a better place." I also heard he is now living in paradise, and I'll see him again. None of that helped! It would anger me so much! The better place for my nineteen-year-old son was *here* with us, his family, living his life!

"You were blessed to have a beautiful son for 19 years." I *know* I was blessed by him. I know others are less fortunate than I, but when you lose a child, hearing that is not helpful, it's hurtful. It takes away my right to miss my child, and made me feel guilty for complaining or being sad. I had every right to be sad!

People often told me to call if I needed anything. A person in deep grief doesn't have the wherewithal to make that call. We feel lost, and in despair.

Have you come to a place on your journey where you can recognize some meaning within the loss?

This was a difficult question. I'm five years into my journey, and it's still hard. But I feel like I've done the hard work of grieving. I'm not done and may never be done, but I feel good knowing I've managed to maintain joy in my life and yes, I believe I have found some meaning in the loss. I hate that my son died, I hate that he isn't physically here with us, but I have learned so much from his death. I've learned that suicide is an epidemic of major proportions, and that we as suicide loss survivors have a chance to share our stories and educate people. We can be the messengers who will help to remove the stigma that is associated with suicide. It is up to us to promote awareness and prevention by letting people know that suicide is not a weakness, it isn't a selfish act, and it *is* a disease. We need the courage to step up and correct people when they say "committed suicide." Brenden Did Not commit anything! He Died by suicide, a disease of the brain and mind.

I have also learned more about grief and mourning than I ever expected or wanted to know. It is hard work, but you need to befriend your pain and delve into it in order to start healing. So yes, I am finding meaning in my loss through helping others cope with their grief. I walk alongside them as they share their "love stories" with me and I am with them as they journey through their own grief and find healing and meaning for themselves. I continue to learn from them as well. In doing this, in helping others in whatever small way I can, I honor my son, his memory, and I honor myself.

Tara's husband, Lenny died of colon cancer in August 2009.

They had been married just ten days shy of their twenty-first anniversary.

What have others said or done that you found to be helpful?

In the first months after the death of my husband, what was most helpful was to keep busy with work and supporting our two children. I read a lot about grief and loss and attended a few presentations about loss of a partner.

I appreciated those friends who reached out to simply check in on me as I was isolating myself.

There was a conversation with a woman who was fifteen years older than I was, who had a similar experience fifteen years earlier. I sat with her at a Chamber of Commerce event and had a wonderful conversation about our experiences. This probably had the most impact in giving me hope for healing.

I found it helpful to meet others who were also dealing with the loss of their spouses and were now raising children as a single parent.

I found a small group in which we supported and helped each other.

We spent time simply talking thru emotions and situations we were similarly facing as well as our children's grief and grieving the loss of a partner at the same time.

On the other hand, what wasn't helpful?
I did isolate myself in some parts of my life which evolved into some poor habits. I found myself wallowing in a bit of quiet self-pity.

Having people reminding me that I was "young and will find someone" or let me know that I should find someone else wasn't helpful.

When people would approach with a forlorn look and dramatically ask "How. Are. You. Doing?"

I HATED that!

Have you come to a place on your journey where you can recognize some meaning within the loss?

I am not sure that I have found meaning in the loss itself. I however have learned a lot about myself in accepting the things I cannot change.

Knowing what is important, I have learned to be more patient, more compassionate, a better listener, a better mother, and a better friend.

I have forgiven myself for the mistakes I have made.

I have prioritized my time and try to live fully each day.

How we walk with the broken speaks louder than how we sit with the great. – Bill Bennot

The Beatitudes for Those Who Comfort
Jackie Deems
Used with permission

Blessed are those who do not use tears to measure the true feelings of the bereaved.

Blessed are those who stifle the urge to say, "I understand," when they don't.

Blessed are those who do not expect the bereaved to put in the past someone who is still fresh in their hearts.

Blessed are those who do not have a quick "comforting" answer, preach a sermon, or continually quote scripture after scripture verse to the bereaved in an effort to make them "better."

Blessed are those who do not make judgments on the bereaved's closeness to God by their reaction to the loss of their loved one.

Blessed are those who listen with their hearts, not with their minds.

Blessed are those who allow the bereaved enough time to heal.

Blessed are those who put their uncomfortableness aside to walk with the bereaved.

Blessed are those who do not give unwanted advice.

Blessed are those who understand the worth of each person as a unique individual and do not suggest they can be replaced or forgotten.

Blessed are those who continue to call, visit, and reach out when the crowd has dwindled and the wounded are left standing alone.

Blessed are those who realize the fragility of bereavement and offer the bereaved a loving shoulder to cry on and a compassionate heart.

Chapter 16

Meaning...Purpose...Hope

Our society tells us to get over grief and to move on. But that's just not how it works. There is no timeline for grief. When we go through all Five Areas of healing grief, we can find peace even after the most devastating losses.
—David Kessler, author of Finding Meaning

Grief is not a linear process with a series of steps to be taken. It is normal to find yourself vacillating between all these areas, in some instances, multiple times. The breadth and width of the journey is different for everyone. The relationship, the manner of death and the amount of support available all play into the healing.

The old adage of "time heals all wounds" has some cracks in it. Time alone won't heal all wounds any more than putting a band aid on a broken leg will heal it. Time passing, accompanied by sincere effort to do the hard work of grieving well and choosing to seek and accept support, is what will make the difference.

The five areas of healing grief are:

1. Denial
2. Anger
3. Bargaining
4. Depression
5. Acceptance

And to this, author and speaker, David Kessler has added one more: Meaning.

Meaning is the sixth area of healing grief. He says that meaning can be found in the life of anyone who ever occupied space on this planet or in anyone's heart. It is there if you look for it. The word "meaning" might also be replaced with "hope" or "purpose." There is no timeline or rhythm to the other areas of healing, and the same is true for meaning. However, it is important that we experience all of them before rushing to meaning and ignoring the work of the others. There are no shortcuts for the grief journey. Try as many have, most will find themselves dealing with all that loss and grief require of us for the time that it takes.

I highly recommend Kessler's book, *Finding Meaning*. It is rich with stories of those who have suffered great losses and yet, after coming to a place of acceptance, have moved forward to discover meaning purpose and hope.

Viktor Frankl has done extensive work in this area of healing as well. His insight was born out of the years he spent in Nazi concentration camps. Even there in deplorable conditions, he recognized that even when man is stripped of almost everything, we all still have one thing. That is to choose our attitude and decide how we will move forward. None of us has the power to change what has happened, so we are left with the choice to change ourselves.

Many times as I have sat with someone who is in so much pain after the death of their loved one, I can offer this tiny ray of hope. "What I know to be true, is that this won't always hurt as much as it does right now." These times are not forever...if we are willing to do the hard work of healing and finding meaning.

Meaning comes in many different forms. There is meaning in:

- Knowing that your loved one was able to give the gift of life by being an organ donor.
- Establishing a scholarship in his or her name.
- The time spent with them before their death.
- Becoming a more intentional parent, spouse, or friend.
- Taking on a cause that was important to them.

Often people have found a positive and meaningful way to express their pain and anger over an injustice.

Candace Lightner did just that. In 1980, her thirteen-year-old daughter Cari was struck and killed by a drunk driver. She used her pain, rage, and grief to create MADD, Mothers Against Drunk Drivers. Candace and her team's gallant efforts have helped to save 370,000 lives. In 2000, MADD was responsible for seeing that a federal law was passed to lower the drunk driving limit to .08%. Among other focuses, MADD is also committed to supporting the survivors, families and friends following the crash.

Many factors will play a part in how we process grief. Certain manners of death will most certainly complicate each person's experience. Death by suicide, an overdose, the death of a child, a sudden death, the death of someone we loved but were estranged from, are some of them. The extra pain and trauma that accompanies these is real. Fortunately, there are many stories about those survivors who have accomplished finding their purpose and meaning even then.

Part V

The Resiliency Factor

Chapter 17

The Resiliency Factor
—and the Signs That Guide Us

I have heard the word "resiliency," and have written and talked about "resiliency" quite often in the last year or so. A simple way to describe it would be *the ability to bend without breaking.* I use the analogy of a palm tree, which in the strong winds of a tropical storm, has the ability to bend so far that it literally touches the ground beneath it. Scientists have discovered that not only can palm trees, and bamboo as well, bend to those depths without breaking, but the trees that were healthy before the storm are proven to be even stronger after it passes. What a wonderful correlation as we consider our potential to stand stronger after our own storms. Of course there will be times when we will feel like we didn't bend without breaking and that's ok. It matters more how many times we pick ourselves up and take the next step forward.

Every one of us has already overcome some adversity in our lives. We all have our own stories of difficult times. Some of the storms were short lived while others will be woven through the rest of our lives. Some are behind us, and some are yet to come.

A variety of challenges will continue to test our resiliency. There is illness, whether it be our own or someone we care about. There can be job loss, divorce, family issues, addiction, and of course, death.

In his book, *The Last Lecture*, Randy Pausch said, "Experience is what you get when you didn't get what you wanted." Isn't that true? For me, it seems my greatest lessons were learned in the valleys of my life. It has been in those seasons that I got to know myself better, as I could either choose to give up or stand up. I also found out more about the people in my life, as they either were willing to spend some time with me there—or not.

My hope is that as you read the pages of this book, hearing other people's stories as well as our own, you are able to apply some of what I've shared to your own story. No matter your story, I have every reason to believe that you will also be able to cultivate a resilient spirit.

- So, how do we do that?
- How do we navigate the journey?
- Where do we find the strength to keep going?

For many, it's through our faith in something bigger than ourselves. For my husband and me it is our faith in Jesus and His words. It's believing that God will give us exactly what we need at the right time as we learn to rely on Him to accomplish His purpose in us.

It's believing that God could do something at any moment that could change the direction of our lives, and we don't want to miss it, so we keep moving forward. You might recall His still-small voice very early in my grief that said, "Together you and I will make good come from this." Because God keeps His promises, it is abundantly clear to me that together we have done just that. This spiritual component has been such a huge piece of our healing and resilience.

Of course, other factors can also help us to strengthen our muscle of resilience. Traits such as possessing good problem-solving skills, having social support available and being likely to seek help, are among some of them.

Who and what we surround ourselves with will have an impact on our resiliency.

I want you to go with me now and embark on the *Road to Resiliency*, and let's observe the signs along the way.

YIELD: The first sign is the YIELD sign. Yield to what the challenge is requiring of you. Often it is going to demand your time and energy and ask you to feel the feelings that will frequently arise, often at inopportune times. Set aside time to acknowledge what feelings you are experiencing, and name them. Are you sad, angry, fearful, feeling abandoned, or lonely?

Also yield or pause before you turn to any method you might use to escape the pain. Resist the tendency to "take the edge off" with alcohol, sex, food, work, unhealthy relationships, shopping, or the Internet. In her book, *The Gift of Imperfections*, Brene' Brown talked about the danger in numbing the dark because when we do, we are also numbing the light. It won't serve us well to refuse to tolerate discomfort because the end result means you'll become someone who can no longer sense joy either. Our brains do not have the ability to differentiate between negative and positive emotions. You will simply become numb.

Educate yourself by reading, listening to podcasts, and talking with others who understand. Consider a support group that fits your needs such as Divorce Care, Celebrate Freedom, or a Grief Support Group.

FALLING ROCKS: The next sign is FALLING ROCKS. I mentioned the triggers that befall many people in grief. You can fully expect to be blindsided from time to time. It is very difficult to prepare ahead of time for these falling rocks. There were many times when I was anxious about a pending situation, and then surprised that it really wasn't as difficult as I thought it might be. On the other hand, there were more times when I didn't expect that I would have reacted the way I did. In the loss of loved one by any means, the trigger may be something as simple as a food, a fragrance, a song or just a memory.

I'll give you an example of one of my falling rocks. Timm loved angel food cake, so much so that he learned to make it himself. It wasn't unusual for Dick and I to come home after running errands on a Saturday to find that Timm had baked a cake...ate it ALL...and left the tube pan in the sink. Even when I baked the angel food and placed it over a long - necked bottle to cool, I more than once discovered all the golden brown crust missing when I went to tip it right-side-up to place it on a plate. So, after Timm was gone I quickly learned that I could spare myself some pain if I avoided the cake mix aisle at the grocery store.

These words also capture the concept of "Falling Rocks".

What some don't understand is the
unpredictability of grief.
You can be having a good moment or a good day,
feeling as though healing is running
through your soul.
You catch yourself smiling once more.
And then, in an instant—Boom.
A thought, a scent, a memory...
And you find yourself once again feeling the
Magnitude of all that was lost

You find yourself once again feeling the void that still
has the ability—
To take your breath away

Used with permission
Coach John Polo, known as the Better Not Bitter
Widower lost his young fiancé to cancer.
www.BetterNotBitterWidower.com.

DETOUR: Have you ever come across a DETOUR
sign? All of a sudden, things aren't going as planned.
You're on a different road, not of your choosing. Can
we relate that to the unexpected challenges that we
have all faced? Just like a detour on a road trip, we have
a choice to make. We can either turn around and go
home and never reach our destination or we can
proceed with trepidation and keep moving forward. It
makes us resilient.

REST AREA: Finally, don't speed by the REST AREA.
Take time to breathe, literally! Even as you're reading
this, stop and try this. Sit up tall with your shoulders
back. Close your eyes and slowly breathe in through
your nose as you count to six. Hold for four seconds
and then slowly exhale through your mouth until you
have expelled all the air. Repeat that two to three times,
and then notice how you feel. I often use this for going
to sleep—or at times when I'm driving (with my eyes
open). You could also do it at your desk at work or
while you're standing in line at the store.

Here are some other things you can do at the REST AREA:

- Listen to music that brings you peace
- Take a walk/run/bike ride
- Soak in a warm bath surrounded by candles
- Get a massage
- Read a book
- Go to lunch with a friend who "fills your cup"
- Express gratitude

Observing and adhering to all these signs along the rocky path of loss and grief will only help you to strengthen your own resiliency muscle.

We are pressed on every side from our troubles,
but we are not crushed. We are perplexed,
but not driven to despair.
We are hunted down, but never abandoned by God.
We get knocked down, but we are not destroyed.
2 Corinthians 4: 8–9

I think this sounds a lot like resilience!

Elizabeth Kubler Ross, well known for her research and writing on grief said this, "People are like stained-glass windows. They sparkle and shine when the sun is out, but when the darkness sets in, their beauty is revealed only if there is a light from within."

My hope and prayer for you is that all of us will strive to do the hard work of becoming resilient people who are lit from within. Our world desperately needs that.

Chapter 18

Not Normal...But Better
Changes —Some Good; Others Not

As I am in the midst of finishing this book, the world is experiencing something that no one in this century has before. Covid-19, pandemic, and masks have become household words.

It was as if a switch was turned off and almost everything changed overnight. Non-essential businesses were closed and students finished their current school year by way of "distance learning." Many adults are now working from home. Restaurants are struggling to keep their establishments afloat by way of curbside service with limited seating and social distancing inside. The city playgrounds in many communities are surrounded by bright orange construction fencing. The implications are many and far-reaching.

For me, I am grieving for all those who have gone far too long without receiving the personal support they need after the death of a loved one. For example:

- For an extended time period there have been no groups meeting as churches and all community gathering venues (including grief groups), were closed.
- Yes, with wonderful options like Zoom, Facetime, etc., I am able to see some faces and hear their voices, but it is not the same for any of us.
- I miss the personal connections and the ability to hold their hand and give them a hug.
- Outside of our homes, the best we can do is remain six feet apart, wearing a mask.
- Funerals had initially been restricted to no more than ten people present, six feet apart.
- If their loved ones were residents of a care facility, the family hasn't been allowed to visit at all, except through a pane of glass and talk via phone.
- Many who have become ill enough to need hospitalization are also alone, with no visitors allowed in.

The long-term implications of the collective repressed grief will be with us for years to come.

I'd like to encourage you to think about those you know who have been on their own journey of grief during these challenging times. Isolation is always a factor when you're suffering from a loss and the pandemic has magnified this even more. Even though we see the term "services pending," in an obituary or someplace else, we know that grief isn't 'pending.' Please make it a point to reach out to that someone you know who may really need a listening ear with the understanding that their grief process has been delayed but it didn't just dissipate.

Only God can take all this which is meant to defeat us—and make it good.

We have seen some good coming from this "Twilight Zone" time.

- Families have been able to spend much more time together as their crazy schedules were replaced with family meals.
- We were all made aware of the things we had taken for granted.
- People have taken up new hobbies or are taking some online courses they didn't have time for before.
- We have become more in tune with others' needs and are checking in with a call or text.
- Some families gather via Zoom to celebrate a holiday or a birthday.

- Others have a certain day and time each week for a group to use Zoom to play a card game.
- Many have used these days to up their fitness routine and eat healthier meals.

I tried to follow my own advice for self-care. Taking long, brisk walks and riding my bike have become my way of relieving the stress that I feel. I spend time each morning reading my devotions and Bible. I'm journaling and staying in touch with friends as we gather in open spaces, grateful that we can enjoy our summer season. This is a world-wide event, and I only sense what it is doing to my little corner of this big blue planet. The fear is almost palpable as I encounter others at the grocery store and other places. Masks cover their nose and mouth, but not their eyes. The eyes may display fatigue, worry, and anger, along with fear. People seem hesitant to look at each other, much less speak a word of encouragement or hope. Kindness seems to be waning, replaced by judgment for some who choose not to wear a mask in public.

But, like almost everyone else, we grieve what
seems to have been lost in
all this and wonder what it will mean in the future.
Maybe we don't want to go back to normal, but "to better."

Final Thoughts

I don't know what prompted you to read this book. Maybe you are a friend, a family member or someone who has heard our story at some event in the past. I hope you are glad you read it and it was able to meet a need you may have.

If you are on our own journey of loss and grief, I would want it to bring you hope and encouragement as you move forward. Maybe you feel assured that what you've been experiencing and thinking is more normal than you might have known. I would want you to go forward being gentler and kinder to yourself and confident that God has not left or forsaken you.

For those that aren't in the middle of a grief experience, life proves that you've been there in the past and/or will be in the future. My wish would be that you have learned about how to Come Alongside someone else, better equipped to listen and love without expectations or judgement. May you seek to strengthen your Resiliency muscles for what the future holds.

Whatever your circumstances, I want you to consider living the rest of your life as if you're preparing to answer the question, "What Have You Done Since I Left?" It is that very thought that has been the impetus for me to continue what I've been doing. What we each do to be able to answer that question, if it be asked, will vary. I want my boys to be proud of me. I am blessed to be able to keep their memories alive by telling my story and encouraging others to tell their stories too. I am grateful that what I've learned may serve to ease someone else's pain a bit.

No matter what we lose during a lifetime, be it possessions, positions or people, there is one thing that can't be taken from us. That is our freedom to decide what our attitude is going to be. That decision will either grant us a full and rewarding life that makes a difference or a life lived out with regrets and unhappiness. We each get to choose. Choose well my friend.

Focused on the Goal

I'm not saying that I have this all together, that I have it made. But I am well on my way, reaching out for Christ, who has so wondrously reached out for me. Friends, don't get me wrong: By no means do I count myself an expert in all of this, but I've got my eye on the goal, where God is beckoning us onward – to Jesus. I'm off and running and I'm not turning back.

From The Message Bible
Philippians 3:12-14

Recommendations

Books

- *Recovering from the Losses in Life* by H. Norman Wright
- *A Grace Disguised* by Jerry Sittser
- *Finding Meaning / The Sixth Stage of Grief* by David Kessler
- *Helping Those in Grief: A Guide to Help You Care for Others* by H. Norman Wright
- *It's OK That You're Not OK* by Megan Devine

Websites

- Grief.com
- OptionB.org
- GriefShare.com
- The Better Not Bitter Widower

About the Author

Inspirational speaker and author, Donna Mathiowetz, strives to leave a legacy of hope, healing, and forgiveness by sharing her story of loss, grief, and resiliency.

Donna's programs include speaking to a variety of groups who are coping with personal life-changing losses. She has been a part of community outreach efforts sponsored by funeral homes, churches, women's groups, grief support groups, and beyond. She has also presented to businesses and corporations such as Life Source, Securian Financial, and Keller Williams. Donna also offers a half-day or full-day Resiliency Factor workshop.

Loss enters our lives in many ways, be it through death, declining health, loss of independence, or dreams that never became reality. Donna's own story is a powerful example of how it is possible to not just survive these, but to thrive after loss. She offers hope as she shares her own journey, as well as those of others she has walked beside. After experiencing

Donna's inspiring and heartfelt presentation, audiences will come away with a better understanding of what grief is and hope that it is possible to heal and help others along the way.

Contact her for a virtual or live presentation for your organization or business.

Follow Donna on Facebook or Instagram @ Unfinished by Design.

Contact her by email at Donna@UnfinishedByDesign.com or through her website at UnfinishedByDesign.com